SNAPSHOT

Normandy

CONTENTS

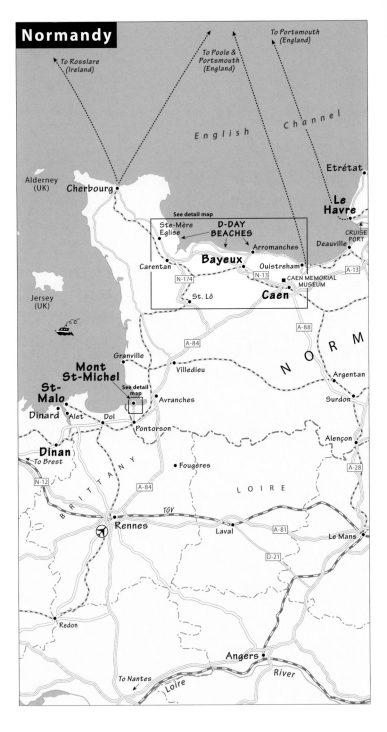

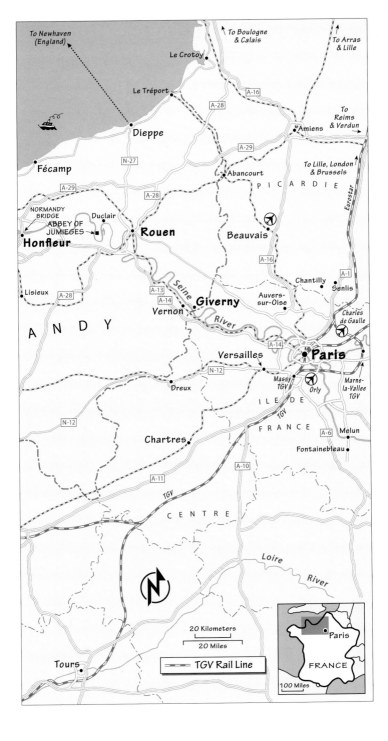

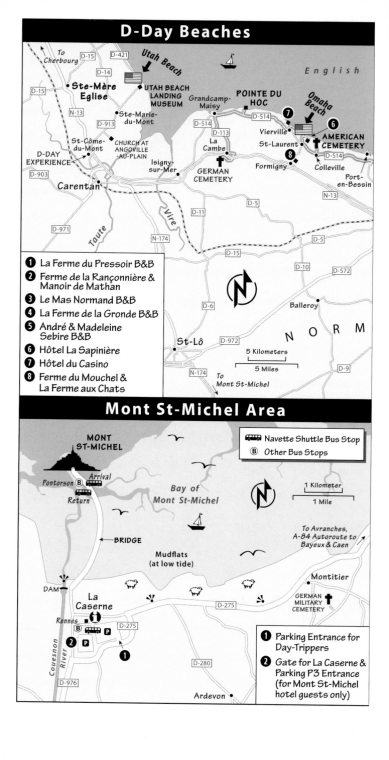

D-Day Beaches

To Cherbourg
D-15
D-421
D-14
Utah Beach
English

Ste-Mère Eglise
D-15
N-13
UTAH BEACH LANDING MUSEUM
Grandcamp-Maisy
POINTE DU HOC
Omaha Beach
❼
❻
AMERICAN CEMETERY

Ste-Marie-du-Mont
D-913
D-514
D-514
Vierville
St-Laurent
❽
Colleville
Port-en-Bessin

St-Côme-du-Mont
CHURCH AT ANGOVILLE-AU-PLAIN
D-113
La Cambe
D-514

D-DAY EXPERIENCE
D-903
Isigny-sur-Mer
GERMAN CEMETERY
Formigny

Carentan
Taute
Vire
D-11
D-5
N-13

D-971
N-174
D-15
D-5
D-10
D-572

N

D-6
Balleroy

St-Lô
D-972
5 Kilometers
5 Miles
N O R M

N-174
To Mont St-Michel
D-9

❶ La Ferme du Pressoir B&B
❷ Ferme de la Rançonnière & Manoir de Mathan
❸ Le Mas Normand B&B
❹ La Ferme de la Gronde B&B
❺ André & Madeleine Sebire B&B
❻ Hôtel La Sapinière
❼ Hôtel du Casino
❽ Ferme du Mouchel & La Ferme aux Chats

Mont St-Michel Area

MONT ST-MICHEL

Navette Shuttle Bus Stop
Ⓑ Other Bus Stops

Pontorson Ⓑ Arrival
Return

Bay of Mont St-Michel

1 Kilometer
1 Mile

N

BRIDGE

To Avranches, A-84 Autoroute to Bayeux & Caen

Mudflats (at low tide)

Montitier

DAM

La Caserne
Rennes Ⓑ P
D-275
D-275

GERMAN MILITARY CEMETERY

Couesnon River
D-976
❷ ❶ P
D-280

Ardevon

❶ Parking Entrance for Day-Trippers
❷ Gate for La Caserne & Parking P3 Entrance (for Mont St-Michel hotel guests only)

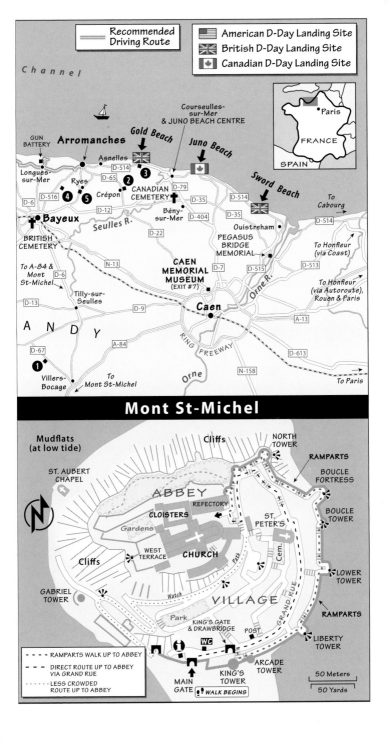

Map Legend

Recommended Driving Route

- 🇺🇸 American D-Day Landing Site
- 🇬🇧 British D-Day Landing Site
- 🇨🇦 Canadian D-Day Landing Site

C h a n n e l

GUN BATTERY

Arromanches

Longues-sur-Mer

Gold Beach

Asnelles
D-514

Ryes
D-65

②

③

Crépon

CANADIAN CEMETERY

D-516

④

⑤

D-12

Courseulles-sur-Mer
& JUNO BEACH CENTRE

Juno Beach

🇨🇦

D-79

Sword Beach

🇬🇧

D-6

✠ **Bayeux**

BRITISH CEMETERY

Seulles R.

Bény-sur-Mer

✠

D-35

D-404

D-514

D-35

Ouistreham

To Cabourg

D-514

D-22

PEGASUS BRIDGE MEMORIAL

To Honfleur (via Coast)
D-513

To A-84 & Mont St-Michel

D-6

N-13

CAEN MEMORIAL MUSEUM
(EXIT #7)

D-7

D-515

To Honfleur (via Autoroute), Rouen & Paris

Tilly-sur-Seulles

D-13

D-9

Caen

Orne R.

A-13

A N D Y

D-67

A-84

RING FREEWAY

①

Villers-Bocage

To Mont St-Michel

Orne

N-158

D-613

To Paris

Mont St-Michel

Mudflats (at low tide)

Cliffs

NORTH TOWER

RAMPARTS

BOUCLE FORTRESS

ST. AUBERT CHAPEL

N

ABBEY

REFECTORY

CLOISTERS

Gardens

ST. PETER'S

BOUCLE TOWER

WEST TERRACE

CHURCH

Cliffs

Path

Cem.

LOWER TOWER

GABRIEL TOWER

Watch

Park

V I L L A G E

GRAND RUE

RAMPARTS

KING'S GATE & DRAWBRIDGE

POST

LIBERTY TOWER

WC

ARCADE TOWER

MAIN GATE

KING'S TOWER

WALK BEGINS

- • • • RAMPARTS WALK UP TO ABBEY
- – – – DIRECT ROUTE UP TO ABBEY VIA GRAND RUE
- ⋯⋯ LESS CROWDED ROUTE UP TO ABBEY

50 Meters

50 Yards

FRANCE
Paris

SPAIN

INTRODUCTION

This Snapshot guide, excerpted from my guidebook *Rick Steves France,* focuses on Normandy—a fascinating region that teems with turning points. For more than a thousand years, legendary figures such as William the Conqueror, Joan of Arc, and General Dwight D. Eisenhower have changed history here. But Normandy is more than invasions and D-Day beaches. Honfleur's gentle harbor inspired the Impressionists, as did Rouen's magnificent cathedral. A thousand-year-old tapestry in Bayeux captures the drama of medieval warfare in a million stitches. On your journey, discover the architectural—and spiritual—marvel of Mont St. Michel, rising above the tidal flats like a mirage.

To help you have the best trip possible, I've included the following topics in this book:

· **Planning Your Time,** with advice on how to make the most of your limited time

· **Orientation,** including tourist information (abbreviated as TI), tips on public transportation, local tour options, and helpful hints

· **Sights** with ratings:

▲▲▲—Don't miss

▲▲—Try hard to see

▲—Worthwhile if you can make it

No rating—Worth knowing about

· **Sleeping and Eating,** with good-value recommendations in every price range

· **Connections,** with tips on trains, buses, and driving

Practicalities, near the end of this book, has information on money, staying connected, hotel reservations, transportation, and more, plus French survival phrases.

To travel smartly, read this little book in its entirety before you go. It's my hope that this guide will make your trip more meaningful and rewarding. Traveling like a temporary local, you'll get the absolute most out of every mile, minute, and dollar.

Bon voyage!

Rick Steves

NORMANDY

Rouen • Honfleur • Bayeux • D-Day Beaches • Mont St-Michel

Sweeping coastlines, half-timbered towns, and thatched roofs decorate the rolling green hills of Normandy (Normandie). Parisians call Normandy "the 21st arrondissement." It's their escape—the nearest beach. Brits consider this area close enough for a weekend escape (you'll notice that the BBC comes through loud and clear on your car radio).

Despite the peacefulness you sense today, the region's history is filled with war. Normandy was founded by Viking Norsemen who invaded from the north, settled here in the ninth century, and gave the region its name. A couple hundred years later, William the Conqueror invaded England from Normandy. His 1066 victory is commemorated in a remarkable tapestry at Bayeux. A few hundred years after that, France's greatest cheerleader, Joan of Arc (Jeanne d'Arc), was convicted of heresy in Rouen and burned at the stake by the English, against whom she rallied France during the Hundred Years' War. And in 1944, Normandy was the site of a WWII battle that changed the course of history.

The rugged, rainy coast of Normandy harbors wartime bunkers and enchanting fishing villages like Honfleur. And, on the border Normandy shares with Brittany, the almost surreal island-abbey of Mont St-Michel rises serene and majestic, oblivious to the tides of tourists.

PLANNING YOUR TIME

For many, Normandy makes the perfect jet-lag antidote: A good first stop for your trip is Rouen, which is a few hours by car or train from Paris' Charles de Gaulle or Beauvais airports. Plan on three nights for a first visit to Normandy: Honfleur, the D-Day beach-

---

Normandy at a Glance

▲▲▲**D-Day Beaches** Atlantic coastline—stretching from Utah Beach in the west to Sword Beach in the east—littered with WWII museums, monuments, and cemeteries left in tribute to the Allied forces who successfully carried out the largest military operation in history: D-Day. See page 58.

▲▲▲**Mont St-Michel** Pretty-as-a-mirage island abbey that once sent pilgrims' spirits soaring—and today does the same for tourists. See page 94.

▲▲**Rouen** Lively city whose old town is a pedestrian haven, mixing a soaring Gothic cathedral, half-timbered houses, and Joan of Arc sights. See page 9.

▲▲**Honfleur** Picturesque port town, located where the Seine greets the English Channel, whose shimmering light once captivated Impressionist painters. See page 28.

▲▲**Bayeux** Six miles from the D-Day beaches and the first city liberated after the D-Day landings, worth a visit for its famous medieval tapestry, enjoyable town center, and awe-inspiring cathedral, beautifully illuminated at night. See page 43.

---

es, and Mont St-Michel each merit an overnight. At a minimum, you'll want a full day for the D-Day beaches and a half-day each in Honfleur, Bayeux, and Mont St-Michel.

If you're driving between Paris and Honfleur, Giverny and Rouen make good detours. The WWII memorial museum in Caen works well as a stop between Honfleur and Bayeux (and the D-Day beaches). Mont St-Michel must be seen early or late to avoid the masses of midday tourists. Dinan, just 45 minutes by car from Mont St-Michel, offers a fine introduction to Brittany. Drivers can enjoy Mont St-Michel as a day trip from Dinan.

Winter travelers should note that many sights on the D-Day beaches and in Bayeux are closed in January. For practical information about travel, current events, concerts, and more in Normandy, see www.normandie-tourisme.fr.

GETTING AROUND NORMANDY

This region is best explored by **car.** If you're driving into Honfleur from the north, take the impressive Normandy Bridge (Pont de Normandie, €6 toll). If you're driving from Mont St-Michel into Brittany, follow my recommended scenic route to the town of St-Malo (see page 111).

NORMANDY

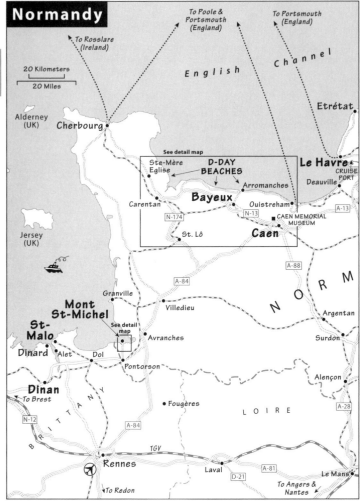

Trains from Paris serve Rouen, Caen, Bayeux, Mont St-Michel (via Pontorson or Rennes), and Dinan, though service between these sights can be frustrating (try linking by bus—see next). Mont St-Michel is a headache by train, except from Paris. Enterprising businesses in Bayeux run shuttles between Bayeux and Mont St-Michel—a great help to those without cars (see page 57).

Buses link Giverny, Honfleur, Arromanches, and Mont St-Michel to train stations in nearby towns (less frequent on Sundays). To plan ahead, visit the websites for Bus Verts (for Le Havre, Honfleur, Bayeux, Arromanches, and Caen, www.busverts.fr), Keolis (for Mont St-Michel, www.destination-montsaintmichel.com), and Tibus or Illenoo (for Dinan and St-Malo, www.tibus.fr

or www.illenoo-services.fr). Bus companies commonly offer good-value and multiride discounts—for example, Bus Verts offers a 20 percent discount on a shareable four-ride ticket.

Another good option is to use an **excursion tour** to link destinations. **Westcapades** provides trips to Mont St-Michel from Dinan and St-Malo.

NORMANDY'S CUISINE SCENE

Normandy is known as the land of the four C's: Calvados, Camembert, cider, and *crème*. The region specializes in cream sauces, organ meats (sweetbreads, tripe, and kidneys—the gizzard salads are great), and seafood *(fruits de mer)*. You'll see *crêperies* offering

Camembert Cheese

This cheap, soft, white, Brie-like cheese is sold all over France (and America) in distinctive, round wooden containers. The Camembert region has long been known for its cheese, but local legend has it that today's cheese got its start in the French Revolution, when a priest on the run was taken in by Marie Harel, a Camembert farm woman. The priest repaid the favor by giving her the secret formula for his hometown cheese—Brie.

From cow to customer, Camembert takes about three weeks to make. High-fat milk from Norman cows is curdled with rennet, ladled into round, five-inch molds, sprinkled with Penicillium camemberti bacteria, and left to dry. In the first three days, the cheese goes from the cow's body temperature to room temperature to refrigerator cool (50 degrees). Two weeks later, the ripened and aged cheese is wrapped in wooden bands and labeled for market. Like wines, Camembert cheese is controlled by government regulations and must bear the "A.O.C." (Appellation d'Origine Contrôlée) stamp of approval.

inexpensive and good-value meals everywhere. A galette is a savory buckwheat crêpe enjoyed as a main course; a crêpe is sweet and eaten for dessert.

Dairy products are big, too. Local cheeses are Camembert (mild to very strong; see sidebar), Brillat-Savarin (buttery), Livarot (spicy and pungent), Pavé d'Auge (spicy and tangy), and Pont l'Evêque (earthy).

What, no local wine? *Eh oui,* that's right. Here's how to cope. Fresh, white Muscadet wines are made nearby (in western Loire); they're cheap and a good match with much of Normandy's cuisine. But Normandy is proud of its many apple-based beverages. You can't miss the powerful Calvados apple brandy or the Bénédictine brandy (made by local monks). The local dessert, *trou Normand,* is apple sorbet swimming in Calvados. The region also produces three kinds of alcoholic apple ciders: *Cidre* can be *doux* (sweet), *brut* (dry), or *bouché* (sparkling—and the strongest). You'll also find bottles of Pommeau, a tasty blend of apple juice and Calvados (sold in many shops), as well as *poiré,* a tasty pear cider. And don't leave Normandy without sampling a *kir Normand,* a mix of crème de cassis and cider. Drivers in Normandy should be on the lookout for *Route du Cidre* signs (with a bright red apple); this tourist trail leads you to small producers of handcrafted cider and brandy.

Rouen

This 2,000-year-old city mixes Gothic architecture, half-timbered houses, and contemporary bustle like no other place in France.

Busy Rouen (roo-ahn) is France's fifth-largest port and Europe's biggest food exporter (mostly wheat and grain). Its cobbled old town is a delight to wander.

Rouen was a regional capital during Roman times, and France's second-largest city in medieval times (with 40,000 residents—only Paris had more). In the ninth century, the Normans made the town their capital. William the Conqueror called it home before moving to England. Rouen walked a political tightrope between England and France for centuries and was an English base during the Hundred Years' War. Joan of Arc was burned here (in 1431).

Rouen's historic wealth was built on its wool industry and trade—for centuries, it was the last bridge across the Seine River before the Atlantic. In April 1944, as America and Britain weakened German control of Normandy prior to the D-Day landings, Allied bombers destroyed 50 percent of Rouen. Although the industrial suburbs were devastated, most of the historic core survived, keeping Rouen a pedestrian haven.

PLANNING YOUR TIME

If you want a dose of a smaller—yet lively—French city, Rouen is an easy day trip from Paris, with convenient train connections to Gare St. Lazare (nearly hourly, 1.5 hours). For a memorable day trip from Paris, combine Rouen with Giverny.

If you're planning to rent a car as you leave Paris, save headaches by taking the train to Rouen and picking up a rental car there (spend a quiet night in Rouen and pick up your car the next morning). From Paris you can also take an early train to Rouen, pick up a car, stash your bags in it, leave it in the secure rental lot at the train station, and visit Rouen before heading out to explore Normandy (for car-rental companies, see "Helpful Hints," later). This plan also works in reverse—drop your car in Rouen and visit the city before taking a train to Paris.

Those relying on public transportation can visit Rouen on the way from Paris to other Normandy destinations, thanks to the good bus and train service (see under "Arrival in Rouen, By Train" for bag storage).

Orientation to Rouen

Although Paris embraces the Seine, Rouen ignores it. The area we're most interested in is bounded by the river to the south, the Museum of Fine Arts (Esplanade Marcel Duchamp) to the north, Rue de la République to the east, and Place du Vieux Marché to the west. It's a 20-minute walk from the train station to the Notre-Dame Cathedral, and everything else of interest is within a 10-minute walk of the cathedral.

TOURIST INFORMATION

The TI faces the cathedral and rents €5 audioguides covering the cathedral, Rouen's historic center, and the history of Joan of Arc in Rouen (though this book's self-guided walk is plenty for most). If driving, get information about the Route of the Ancient Abbeys (TI open Mon-Sat 9:00-19:00, Sun 9:30-12:30 & 14:00-18:00; Oct-April Mon-Sat 9:30-12:30 & 14:00-18:00, closed Sun; 25 Place de la Cathédrale, tel. 02 32 08 32 40, www.rouentourisme. com).

ARRIVAL IN ROUEN

By Train: Rue Jeanne d'Arc cuts straight from Rouen's train station through the town center to the Seine River. Day-trippers can **walk** from the station down Rue Jeanne d'Arc toward Rue du Gros Horloge—a busy pedestrian mall in the medieval center and near the starting point of my self-guided walk. There's no bag storage at the train station, but the Holibag service lets you store bags at a handful of businesses in central Rouen (tel. 02 35 76 47 80, www. holibag.io).

Rouen's **subway** (Métrobus) whisks travelers from under the train station to the Palais de Justice in one stop (€1.70 for 1 hour; buy tickets from machines one level underground, then validate ticket on subway two levels down; subway direction: Technopôle or Georges Braque). Returning to the station, take a subway in direction: Boulingrin and get off at Gare-Rue Verte.

Taxis (to the right as you exit station) will take you to any of my recommended hotels for about €10.

By Car: Finding the city center from the autoroute is tricky. Follow signs for *Centre-Ville* and *Rive Droite* (right bank). If you get turned around (likely, because of the narrow, one-way streets), aim toward the highest cathedral spires you spot.

As you head toward the center, you should see signs for *P&R Relais*. These are tram stops outside the core where you can park for free, then hop on a tram into town (€1.70 each way). In the city, you can park on the street (metered 8:00-19:00, free overnight), or pay for more secure parking in one of many well-signed underground lots (€14/day; see map on page 12 for locations). For day-trippers taking my self-guided walk of Rouen, the garage under Place du Vieux Marché (Parking Vieux Marché) is best. For those staying overnight, Parking Cathédrale–Office du Tourisme (between the cathedral and the river) is handy.

When leaving Rouen, head for the riverfront road, where autoroute signs will guide you to Paris or to Le Havre and Caen (for D-Day beaches and Honfleur). If you're following the Route of Ancient Abbeys from here, see page 24.

HELPFUL HINTS

Closed Days: Many Rouen sights are closed midday (12:00-14:00), and most museums are closed on Tuesdays. The cathedral doesn't open until 14:00 on Monday, and the Joan of Arc Church is closed Friday and Sunday mornings.

Market Days: The best open-air market is on Place St. Marc, a few blocks east of St. Maclou Church. It's filled with antiques and other good stuff (all day Tue, Fri, and Sat; Sun is best but closes by 13:30). A smaller market is on Place du Vieux Marché, near the Joan of Arc Church (Tue-Sun until 13:30, closed Mon).

Supermarket: A big **Monoprix** is on Rue du Gros Horloge (groceries at the back, Mon-Sat 8:30-21:00, Sun 9:00-13:00).

Cathedral of Light: In summer, Rouen's cathedral generally sports a dazzling light show on its exterior after dark (June-Aug at 23:00, Sept at 22:00).

Wi-Fi: You'll find Wi-Fi at several cafés within a few blocks of the train station on Rue Jeanne d'Arc.

Taxi: Call **Les Taxi Blancs** at 02 35 61 20 50.

Car Rental: Agencies with offices in the train station include **Europcar** (tel. 02 35 88 21 20), **Avis** (tel. 02 35 88 60 94), and **Hertz** (tel. 02 35 70 70 71). All are closed Sunday and for lunch (Mon-Sat 12:30-14:00).

SNCF Boutique: For train tickets, visit the SNCF office at the corner of Rue aux Juifs and Rue Eugène Boudin (Mon 12:30-19:00, Tue-Sat 10:00-19:00, closed Sun).

Rouen Walk

On this 1.5-hour self-guided walk, you'll see the essential Rouen sights (all but the Joan of Arc Museum and Bell Tower Panorama are free) and experience the city's pedestrian-friendly streets. This walk is designed for day-trippers coming by train, but works just as

NORMANDY

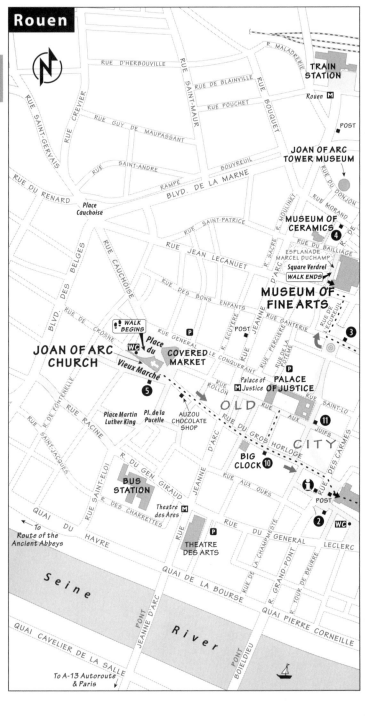

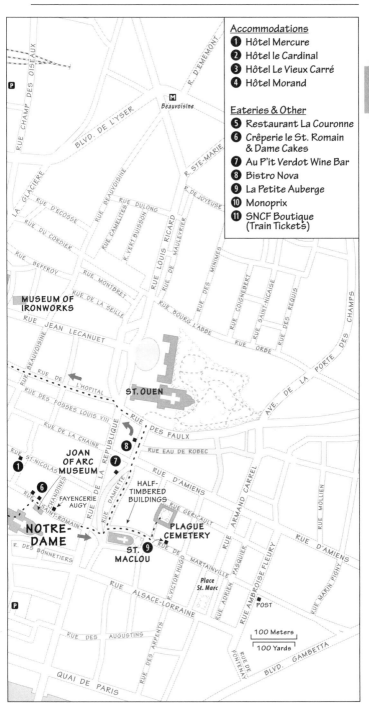

<u>Accommodations</u>
1. Hôtel Mercure
2. Hôtel le Cardinal
3. Hôtel Le Vieux Carré
4. Hôtel Morand

<u>Eateries & Other</u>
5. Restaurant La Couronne
6. Crêperie le St. Romain & Dame Cakes
7. Au P'it Verdot Wine Bar
8. Bistro Nova
9. La Petite Auberge
10. Monoprix
11. SNCF Boutique (Train Tickets)

well for drivers (ideally, park at the underground garage at Place du Vieux Marché, where the walk begins).

We'll stroll the length of Rue du Gros Horloge to Notre-Dame Cathedral, visit the plague cemetery (Aître St. Maclou), pass the church of St. Ouen, and end at the Museum of Fine Arts, a short walk back to the train station or parking lot. The map on the previous page highlights our route.

• *If arriving by train, walk down Rue Jeanne d'Arc and turn right on Rue du Guillaume le Conquérant (notice the Gothic Palace of Justice building across Rue Jeanne d'Arc—we'll get to that later). This takes you to the back door of our starting point...*

▲Place du Vieux Marché

Stand in the small garden near the entrance of the Joan of Arc Church. Find a spot above the tall aluminum cross for striking views of the church. Surrounded by half-timbered buildings, this old market square houses a cute, covered produce-and-fish market, a park commemorating Joan of Arc's burning, and a modern church named after her. That towering cross marks the spot where Rouen publicly punished and executed people. The pillories stood here, and during the Revolution, the town's guillotine made 800 people "a foot shorter at the top." In 1431, Joan of Arc—only 19 years old—was burned right here. Find her flaming statue (built into the wall of the church, facing the cross). As the flames engulfed her, an English soldier said, "Oh my God, we've killed a saint." Nearly 500 years later, Joan was canonized, and the soldier was proved right.

• *Now step inside...*

▲Joan of Arc Church (Eglise Jeanne d'Arc)

This modern church is a tribute to the young woman who was canonized in 1920 and later became the patron saint of France. The church, completed in 1979, feels Scandinavian inside and out—another reminder of Normandy's Nordic roots. Sumptuous 16th-century windows, salvaged from a church lost during World War II, were worked into the soft architectural lines. The pointed, stake-like support columns to the right seem fitting for a church dedicated to a woman burned at the stake. This is an uplifting place to be, with a ship's-hull vaulting and sweeping wood ceiling sailing over curved pews and a wall of glass below. Make time to savor this unusual sanctuary.

Cost and Hours: Free, Mon-Thu and Sat 10:00-12:00 & 14:00-18:00, Fri 10:00-12:00, Sun 14:00-17:30, closed during Mass (Sun at 11:00 plus offseason weekdays at 18:30), 50-cent English pamphlet describes the stained-glass scenes. A public WC is 30 yards straight ahead from the church doors.

• *Turn left out of the church.*

Joan of Arc (1412-1431)

The teenager who rallied French soldiers to drive out English invaders was the illiterate daughter of a humble farmer. One summer day, in her dad's garden, 13-year-old Joan heard a heavenly voice accompanied by bright light. It was the first of several saints (including Michael, Margaret, and Catherine) to talk to her during her short life.

In 1429, the young girl was instructed by the voices to save France from the English. Dressed in men's clothing, she traveled to see the king and predicted that the French armies would be defeated near Orléans—as they were. King Charles VII equipped her with an ancient sword and a banner that read "Jesus, Maria," and sent her to rally the troops.

Soon "the Maid" (la Pucelle) was bivouacking amid rough soldiers, riding with them into battle, and suffering an arrow wound to the chest—all while liberating the town of Orléans. On July 17, 1429, she held her banner high in the cathedral of Reims as Charles was officially proclaimed king of a resurgent France.

Joan and company next tried to retake Paris (1429), but the English held out. She suffered a crossbow wound through the thigh, and her reputation of invincibility was tarnished. During a battle at Compiègne (1430), she was captured and turned over to the English for £10,000. The English took her to Rouen, where she was chained by the neck inside an iron cage while the local French authorities (allied with the English) plotted against her. The Inquisition—insisting that Joan's voices were "false and diabolical"—tried and sentenced her to death for being a witch and a heretic.

On May 30, 1431, Joan of Arc was tied to a stake on Rouen's old market square (Place du Vieux Marché). She yelled, "Rouen! Rouen! Must I die here?" Then they lit the fire; she fixed her eyes on a crucifix and died chanting, "Jesus, Jesus, Jesus."

After Joan died, her place in history was slowly rehabilitated. French authorities proclaimed her trial illegal (1455), and she quickly became the most important symbol of French nationhood. Over the centuries, prominent writers and artists were inspired by her, politicians co-opted her fame for their own purposes, and common people rallied around her idealized image. Finally, the Catholic Church beatified (1909) and canonized her (1920) as St. Joan of Arc.

Ruined Church and Julia Child

As you leave the church, you're stepping over the ruins of a 15th-century church (destroyed during the French Revolution). The charming half-timbered building just beyond—overflowing with flags and geraniums—is the recommended Restaurant La Couronne, reputedly the oldest restaurant in France. It was here, in

1949, that American chef and author Julia Child ate her first French meal, experiencing a culinary epiphany that changed her life (and the eating habits of a generation of Americans). By the restaurant's front door find historic photos of happy diners, including Julia.

• *Leave the square with the church on your left and join the busy pedestrian street, Rue du Gros Horloge. An important thoroughfare in Roman times, it's been the city's main shopping street since the Middle Ages. A block up on your right (at #163) is Rouen's most famous chocolate shop.*

Auzou and Houses That Lean Out

The friendly *chocolatiers* at Auzou would love to tempt you with their chocolate-covered almond "tears *(larmes)* of Joan of Arc." Although you must resist touching the chocolate fountain, you are welcome to taste a tear (delicious). The first one is free; a small bag costs about €9.50.

Before moving on, notice the architecture. The higher floors of the Auzou house lean out, evidence that the building dates from before 1520, when such street-crowding construction was prohibited. (People feared that houses leaning over the street like this would block breezes and make the city more susceptible to disease.) Look around the corner and down the lane behind the Auzou building to see a fine line of half-timbered Gothic facades. Study the house next to Auzou, at #161. You can tell it was built after 1520 (because its facade is flat) and that it's Renaissance (because of the characteristic carved wooden corner-posts). We'll see more houses like this later on our walk.

• *Your route continues past a medieval McDonald's to busy **Rue Jeanne d'Arc**. Pause here and look both ways. With the 19th-century Industrial Age, France expanded its transportation infrastructure. A train line connecting Paris to Rouen arrived in the early 1840s, and major roads like this were plowed through to get traffic efficiently to the station. The facades here date from the 1860s and are in the Haussmann style so dominant in Paris in that era.*

Cross the street and continue straight to the...

▲Great Clock (Gros Horloge)

This impressive, circa-1528 Renaissance clock, the Gros Horloge (groh or-lohzh), decorates the former City Hall. Originally, the clock had only an hour hand but no minute hand. In the 16th century, an hour hand offered sufficient precision; minute hands became necessary only in a later, faster-paced age (forget second hands). The silver orb above the clock makes one revolution in 29 days. (The cycle of the moon let people know the tides—of practical value here as Rouen was a seaport.) The town medallion (sculpted into the stone below the clock) features a sacrificial lamb, which has both religious meaning (Jesus is the Lamb of God) and

The Hundred Years' War (1336-1453)

It would take a hundred years to explain all the causes, battles, and political maneuverings of this century-plus of warfare between France and England. Here's the Hundred Years' War in 100 seconds:

In 1300, before the era of the modern nation-state, the borders between France and England were fuzzy. French-speaking kings had ruled England, English kings owned the south of France, and English merchants dominated trade in the north. Dukes and lords in both countries were aligned more along family lines than by national identity. When the French king died without a male heir (1328), both France and England claimed the crown, and the battle was on.

England invaded the more populous France (1345) and—thanks to skilled archers using armor-penetrating longbows—won big battles at Crécy (1346) and Poitiers (1356). Despite a truce, roving bands of English mercenaries stayed behind and supported themselves by looting French villages. The French responded with guerrilla tactics.

In 1415, with Henry V's big victory at Agincourt, the English took still more territory. But rallied by the heavenly visions of young Joan of Arc, the French slowly drove the invaders out. Paris was liberated in 1436, and when Bordeaux fell to French forces (1453), the fighting ended without a treaty.

commercial significance (wool was the source of Rouen's wealth). The clock's artistic highlight fills the underside of the arch (walk underneath and stretch your back), with the "Good Shepherd" and loads of sheep.

Bell Tower Panorama: To see the inner workings of the clock and an extraordinary panorama over Rouen and its cathedral, climb the clock tower's 100 steps. You'll tour several rooms with the help of a friendly, 40-minute audioguide and learn about life in Rouen when the tower was built. The big one- and two-ton bells ring on the hour—a deafening experience if you're in the tower. Don't miss the 360-degree view outside from the very top (€7, includes audioguide, Tue-Sun 10:00-13:00 & 14:00-19:00, shorter hours off-season, closed Mon year-round).

• *Walk under the Gros Horloge and continue straight a half-block, then take a one-block detour left (up Rue Thouret) to see the...*

Palace of Justice (Palais de Justice)

Rouen is the capital of Normandy, and this impressive building is its parliament. The section on the left is the oldest, in Flamboyant Gothic style dating from 1550. Normandy was an independent little country from 911 to 1204, and since then, while a part of France, it's had an independent spirit and has enjoyed a bit of autonomy.

Behind you is the historic Rue aux Juifs (Street of the Jews)—a reminder that this was the Jewish quarter from the 10th century until the early 14th century, when the Jews were expelled from France. Their homes were destroyed and the city took their land. Later, the empty real estate was used for the parliament.

• *Double back and continue up Rue du Gros Horloge. In a block, high on the left, you'll see a stone plaque dedicated to hometown hero **Cavelier de la Salle**, who explored the mouth of the Mississippi River, claimed the state of Louisiana for France, and was assassinated in Texas in 1687. Soon you'll reach...*

▲▲Notre-Dame Cathedral (Cathédrale Notre-Dame)

This cathedral is a landmark of art history. You're seeing essentially what Claude Monet saw as he painted 30 different studies of this frilly Gothic facade at various times of day.  Using the physical building only as a rack upon which to hang light, mist, dusk, and shadows, Monet was capturing "impressions." One of these paintings is in Rouen's Museum of Fine Arts; others are at the Orsay Museum in Paris. Find the plaque showing one of the paintings (in the corner of the square, about 30 paces to your right if exiting the TI).

Cost and Hours: Free, Tue-Sun 9:00-19:00 (Nov-March closed 12:00-14:00), Mon 14:00-19:00; Mass: Tue-Sat at 10:00, July-Aug also at 18:00, Sun and holidays at 8:30, 10:30, and 12:00.

Visiting the Cathedral

There's been a church on this site for more than a thousand years. Charlemagne honored it with a visit in the eighth century before the Vikings sacked it a hundred years later. The building you see today was constructed between the 12th and 14th centuries, though lightning strikes, wars (the cathedral was devastated in WWII fighting), and other destructive forces meant constant rebuilding.

Central Facade: Look up at the elaborate, soaring **facade,** with bright statues on either side of the central portal—later, we'll meet some of their friends face-to-face inside the cathedral. The facade is another fine Rouen example of Flamboyant Gothic, and the dark spire, soaring nearly 500 feet high, is awe-inspiring. Why such a big cathedral here? Until the 1700s, Rouen was the second-largest city in France—rich from its wool trade and its booming port. On summer evenings, there's usually a colorful light show on the cathedral's facade (see "Helpful Hints," earlier).

Above the **main door** is a marvelous depiction of the Tree of Jesse. Jesse, King David's father, is shown reclined, resting his head on his hand, looking nonplussed. The tree grows from Jesse's back; the figures sprouting from its branches represent the lineage of Jesus. Many statues on the facade are headless. In 1562, during the French Wars of Religion, Protestant iconoclasts held the city for six months—more than enough time to deface the church.

• *Head inside.*

Cathedral Interior: Look down the center of the **nave.** This is a classic Gothic nave—four stories of pointed-arch arcades, the top filled with windows to help illuminate the interior. Today, the interior is lighter than intended because clear glass has replaced the original colored glass (destroyed over the centuries by angry Protestants, horrible storms, changing tastes, and WWII bombs).

Circle counterclockwise around the church, starting down the right aisle. The side chapels and windows, each dedicated to a different saint, display the changing styles through the centuries. You may find photos halfway down on the right that show WWII bomb damage to the cathedral.

At the high altar, look across and up at the north transept **rose window,** which dates from around 1300. It survived a hurricane in 1683. During World War II the glass was taken out, but the original stone tracery did not survive. On the right (in the south transept) is a **chapel dedicated to Joan of Arc.** Its focal point is a touching statue of the saint being burned. The chapel's modern 1956 windows replaced those destroyed in the war.

Passing through an iron gate after the high altar, you come to several **stone statues.** Each is "bolted" to the wall—as they originally were in their niches high above the street centuries ago. These figures were lifted from the facade during a cleaning and provide a rare chance to stand toe-to-toe with a medieval statue.

Several **stone tombs** on your left date from when Rouen was the Norman capital. The first tomb is for Rollo, the first duke of Normandy who died about 932 (he's also the great-great-great-great grandfather of William the Conqueror, seventh duke of Normandy, c. 1028). Rollo was chief of the first gang of Vikings (the original "Normans") who decided to settle here. Called the Father of Normandy, Rollo died at the age of 80, but he is portrayed on his tomb as if he were 33 (as was the fashion, because Jesus died at that age). Thanks to later pillage and plunder, only Rollo's femur is inside the tomb.

And speaking of body parts, the next tomb once contained the heart of English King **Richard the Lionheart,** famous for his military exploits in the Third Crusade (he died in 1199). Over the years, people forgot about the heart, and it was only rediscovered in 1838. It was eventually analyzed by forensic scientists, who concluded that the king had died from a festering arrow wound (not poison, as popularly thought).

Smile at the cute angels on your right and circle behind the altar. The beautiful **windows** with bold blues and reds are generally from the 13th century. Opposite Richard the Lionheart's tomb is a fine window dedicated to St. Julian, patron of hoteliers and travelers (with pane-by-pane descriptions in English on an easel below).

Continue a few paces, then look up to the **ceiling** over the nave (directly above Rollo's femur). You can see the lighter-colored patchwork where, in 1999, a fierce winter storm caused a spire to crash through the roof.

• *Exit while you can, through the side door of the north transept. (If the door is closed, leave through the main entrance, turn right, then loop back alongside the church.)*

North Transept Facade: Outside, look back at the **facade** over the door of the north transept. The fine carved tympanum (the area over the door) shows a graphic Last Judgment. Jesus stands between the saved (on the left) and the damned (on the right). Notice the devil grasping a miser, who clutches a bag of coins. On the far right, look for the hellish hot tub, where even a bishop (pointy hat) is eternally in hot water. And is it my imagination, or are those saved souls on the far left high-fiving each other?

Most of the facade has been cleaned—blasted with jets of water—but the limestone carving is still black. It's too delicate to survive the hosing. A more expensive laser cleaning has begun, and the result is astonishing.

• *From this courtyard, a gate deposits you on a traffic-free street facing the elegant Art Nouveau facade of the recommended Dame Cakes tea shop. This was originally the **workshop** of the church's lead 19th-century craftsman, Ferdinand Marrou. To showcase his work, he fashioned the wrought iron on this door as well as the fine touches inside.*

Turn right and walk along the appealing Rue St. Romain.

Spire View: In a short distance, look up through an opening above the entrance to the Joan of Arc Museum and gaze back at the cathedral's prickly **spire.** Made of cast iron in the late 1800s—about the same time Gustave Eiffel was building his tower in Paris—the spire is, at 490 feet, the tallest in France. You can also see the smaller (green) spires—one of which was blown over in that violent 1999 storm and crashed—all 30 tons of it—through the roof to the cathedral floor. Replaced in 2013, you can bet it's now securely bolted down.

• *To learn more about Rouen's most famous figure, consider touring the...*

▲Joan of Arc Museum (Historial Jeanne d'Arc)

Rouen's Archbishop's Palace, where in 1431 Joan of Arc was tried and sentenced to death, now hosts a multimedia experience that tells her story. Equipped with headphones, you'll walk for 75 minutes through a series of rooms, each with a brief video presentation that tries very hard to teach and entertain. Your tour ends in the Officialité—the room where the trial took place. You're then set free to explore exhibits examining the role Joan of Arc has played in French culture over the centuries. The complete experience is entertaining and informative, but slow-moving—both kids and adults may find it a little boring.

Cost and Hours: €9.50, required tours depart on the quarter-hour Tue-Sun from 10:00, last tour generally at 17:15, closed 12:00-13:00 and Mon year-round, 7 Rue St. Romain, tel. 02 35 52 48 00, www.historial-jeannedarc.fr.

• *From the museum, continue down atmospheric Rue St. Romain. At #26, find the shop marked...*

Fayencerie Augy

Monsieur Augy and his family welcome shoppers to browse his studio/gallery/shop and see Rouen's earthenware "china" being made in the traditional faience style (Mon-Sat 10:00-19:00, closed Sun, shipping available, 26 Rue St. Romain, www.fayencerie-augy.com). First, the clay is molded and fired. Then it's dipped in white enamel, dried, lovingly hand painted, and fired a second time. Rouen was the first city in France to make this colorfully glazed faience earthenware. In the 1700s, the town had 18 factories churning out the popular product. For more faience, visit the local Museum of Ceramics (see "Sights in Rouen").

• *Peer down Rue des Chanoines (next to Augy) for a skinny example of the higgledy-piggledy streets common in medieval Rouen. Back on Rue St. Romain, walk along the massive Archbishop's Palace, which (after crossing Rue de la République) leads to the fancy...*

St. Maclou Church (Eglise St. Maclou)

This church's unique, bowed facade is textbook Flamboyant Gothic. Notice the flame-like tracery decorating its gable. Because this was built at the very end of the Gothic age—and construction took many years—the carved wooden doors are from the next age: the Renaissance (c. 1550). Study the graphic Last Judgment above the doors, and imagine the mindset of the frightened parishioners who worshiped here. If it's open, the bright and airy interior is worth a quick peek.

• *Leaving the church, turn right, and then take another right (giving the little boys on the corner wall a wide berth). Wander past a fine wall of half-timbered buildings fronting Rue Martainville, to the back end of St. Maclou Church.*

Half-Timbered Buildings

Because the local stone—a chalky limestone from the cliffs of the Seine River—was of poor quality (your thumbnail is stronger), and because local oak was plentiful, half-timbered buildings became a Rouen specialty from the 14th through 19th century. There are still 2,000 half-timbered buildings in town; about 100 date from before 1520. Cantilevered floors were standard until the early 1500s. These top-heavy designs made sense: City land was limited, property taxes were based on ground-floor square footage, and the cantilevering minimized unsupported spans on upper floors. The oak beams provided the structural skeleton of the building, which was then filled in with a mix of clay, straw, or whatever was available.

Until the Industrial Age, this was the textile district where cloth was processed, dyed, and sold. When that industry moved across the river in the 19th century, the neighborhood was mothballed and forgotten. After World War II it was recognized as historic and preserved. Eventually rents went up, and gentrification crept in.

• *A block after the church, on the left at 186 Rue Martainville, a short lane leads to the...*

▲Plague Cemetery (Aître St. Maclou)

During the great plagues of the Middle Ages, as many as two-thirds of the people in this parish died. For the decimated community, dealing with the corpses was an overwhelming task. This half-timbered courtyard (c. 1520, free to enter, daily 9:00-18:00) was a mass grave, an ossuary where the bodies were "processed." Bodies were dumped into the grave (an open pit where the well is now) and drenched in liquid lime to help speed decomposition. Later, the bones were stacked in alcoves above the once-open arcades that line this courtyard. Notice the colonnades with their ghoulish carvings of gravediggers' tools, skulls, crossbones, and characters doing the "dance of death." In this *danse macabre,* Death, the great equalizer, grabs people of all social classes. As you leave, spy the dried black cat (in tiny glass case to the left of the door). Perhaps to overcome evil, it was buried during the building's construction.

Nearby: Farther down Rue Martainville, at Place St. Marc, a colorful market is lively Sunday until about 13:30 and all day Tuesday, Friday, and Saturday.

• *Our tour is over. To return to the* **train station** *or reach the* **Museum of Fine Arts** *directly, turn right from the boneyard, then right again at the little boys (onto Rue Damiette), and hike up a pleasing antique row to the vertical St. Ouen Church (a seventh-century abbey turned*

15th-century church; fine park behind). Turn left when you see St. Ouen Church and continue down traffic-free Rue de l'Hôpital (which becomes Rue Ganterie). Turn right on Rue de l'Ecureuil to find the museum directly ahead. To continue to the train station, turn left onto Rue Jean-Lecanuet, then right onto Rue Jeanne d'Arc.

Sights in Rouen

These museums, all within blocks of one another, are all free, closed on Tuesdays, and never crowded.

▲Museum of Fine Arts (Musée des Beaux-Arts)

Paintings from many periods are beautifully displayed in this overlooked two-floor museum, including works by Caravaggio, Peter Paul Rubens, Paolo Veronese, Jan Steen, Velázquez, Théodore Géricault, Jean-Auguste-Dominique Ingres, Eugène Delacroix, and several Impressionists. With its free admission and calm interior, this museum is worth a short visit for the Impressionists and a surgical hit of a few other key artists. The museum café is good for a peaceful break.

Cost and Hours: Free, €11 for frequent and impressive special exhibitions—check website; open Wed-Mon 10:00-18:00, closed Tue; bag check available, peaceful café, a few blocks below train station at Esplanade Marcel Duchamp, tel. 02 35 71 28 40, www.musees-rouen-normandie.fr.

Visiting the Museum: Pick up the essential museum map at the info desk as you enter, then climb the grand staircase that divides the museum into two wings.

Turning right when you reach the second floor, you'll pass through a few rooms, then start seeing some names you recognize: Ingres and Jacques-Louis David (Room 2.21) and then a good collection of works by Géricault (Room 2.22). Turn left into Room 2.33, with one of Monet's famous paintings of the Rouen cathedral facade. Now loop through this wing to enjoy scenes inspired by Normandy's landscape and works by Impressionist greats (Monet, Sisley, Pissarro, Renoir, Degas, and Corot). Make a point to appreciate beautiful paintings by Impressionists whose names you may not recognize. Room 2.25 showcases a scene of Rouen's busy port in 1855.

Paintings on the other side of the grand staircase are devoted to French painters from the 17th and 18th centuries (Boucher, Fragonard, and Poussin) and Italian works, including several by Veronese. A gripping Caravaggio canvas (Room 2.4), depicting the flagellation of Christ, demands attention with its dramatic lighting and realistic faces.

Stairs at the rear, near the Caravaggio, lead down to an intriguing collection of works by 16th-century Dutch and Belgian artists and temporary exhibits. On the other side of the first floor, pass through the bookstore to find a collection of modern paintings: several by hometown boy Raymond Duchamp-Villon (brother of the famous Dadaist Marcel Duchamp), a few colorful Modiglianis, and a grand-scale Delacroix.

Museum of Ironworks (Musée le Secq des Tournelles, a.k.a. Musée de la Ferronnerie)

This deconsecrated church houses iron objects, many of them more than 1,500 years old. Locks, chests, keys, tools, thimbles, coffee grinders, corkscrews, and flatware from centuries ago—virtually anything made of iron is on display. You can duck into the entry area for a glimpse of a medieval iron scene without passing through the turnstile.

Cost and Hours: Free, no English explanations, Wed-Mon 14:00-18:00, closed Tue, behind Museum of Fine Arts at 2 Rue Jacques Villon, tel. 02 35 88 42 92, www.museelesecqdestournelles.fr.

Museum of Ceramics (Musée de la Céramique)

This fine old mansion is filled with examples of Rouen's famous faience earthenware, dating from the 16th to 18th century. There are also examples of Sèvres and Delft wares—but not a word of English.

Cost and Hours: Free, Wed-Mon 14:00-18:00, closed Tue, 1 Rue Faucon, tel. 02 35 07 31 74, www.museedelaceramique.fr.

Joan of Arc Tower (La Tour Jeanne d'Arc)

This massive tower (1204), part of Rouen's brooding castle, was Joan's prison before her execution. Cross the deep moat and find three small floors (and 122 spiral steps) covering tidbits of Rouen's and Joan's history. The top floor gives a good peek at an impressive wood substructure but no views.

Cost and Hours: Free, Wed-Sat and Mon 10:00-12:30 & 14:00-18:00, Sun 14:00-18:30, closed Tue, one block uphill from the Museum of Fine Arts on Rue du Bouvreuil, tel. 02 35 98 16 21, www.tourjeannedarc.fr.

NEAR ROUEN
The Route of the Ancient Abbeys
(La Route des Anciennes Abbayes)

This driving route—punctuated with medieval abbeys, apples, cherry trees, and Seine River views—provides a pleasing detour for those with cars connecting Rouen and Honfleur or the D-Day beaches. The only "essential" stop on this drive is the Abbey of Jumièges.

From Rouen, follow the Seine along its right bank and track signs carefully for D-982 to Duclair. Fifteen minutes west of Rouen, drivers can stop to admire the gleaming Romanesque church at the **Abbey of St. Georges de Boscherville** (skip the abbey grounds). This perfectly intact and beautiful church makes for interesting comparisons with the ruined church at Jumièges. The café across from the church is good for lunch or drinks.

Leaving Duclair, follow D-65 to Jumièges. Here you'll find the **Abbey of Jumièges,** a spiritual place for lovers of evocative ruins (worth ▲; €6.50, helpful English handout, daily mid-April-mid-Sept 9:30-18:30, shorter hours off-season, ask to borrow the detailed English booklet or pay €7 for the well-done *Itineraries* book; a free app to visit the abbey using 3-D images is available—see website; tel. 02 35 37 24 02, www.abbayedejumieges.fr).

Founded in A.D. 654 as a Benedictine abbey, it was leveled by Vikings in the 9th century, then rebuilt by William the Conqueror in the 11th century. This magnificent complex thrived for centuries as Normandy's largest abbey. It was part of the great monastic movement that reestablished civilization in Normandy from the chaos that followed the fall of Rome.

The abbey was destroyed again during the French Revolution, when it was used as a quarry, and it has changed little since then. Today there is no roof, and many walls are entirely gone. But what remains of the abbey's Church of Notre-Dame is awe-inspiring. Study its stark Romanesque facade standing 160 feet high. Stroll down the nave's center; notice the three levels of arches and the soaring rear wall capped by a lantern tower to light the choir. Find a seat in the ruined apse and imagine the church before its destruction. You'll discover brilliant views of the ruins and better appreciate its importance by wandering into the park.

Decent lunch options lie across the street from the abbey, and there's a TI for the village of Jumièges in front of the parking lot.

From near Jumièges you can cross the Seine on the tiny, free, and frequent car ferry, then connect with the A-13 (better)—or continue following the right bank of the Seine and cross at the Pont de Tancarville bridge (€5) or the magnificent Normandy Bridge (Pont de Normandie, €6). By either route allow 45 minutes from Rouen to Jumièges and another 75 minutes to Honfleur, or two more hours to Bayeux.

Sleeping in Rouen

These hotels are perfectly central, within two blocks of Notre-Dame Cathedral.

$$$ Hôtel Mercure*** is a concrete business hotel with a professional staff, a stay-awhile lobby and bar, and 125 well-equipped and thoughtfully appointed rooms. Suites come with views of the cathedral, but are pricey and not much bigger than a double (some rooms with balconies, air-con, elevator, pay parking garage, spendy breakfast, 7 Rue Croix de Fer, tel. 02 35 52 69 52, www.mercure. com, h1301@accor.com).

$$ Hôtel le Cardinal** is a good value with 15 sharp, well-designed rooms, most with point-blank views of the cathedral and all with queen-size beds and modern bathrooms (larger but pricier fourth-floor rooms with balconies and great cathedral views, reception often unstaffed as owners do the cleaning, elevator, 1 Place de la Cathédrale, tel. 02 35 70 24 42, www.cardinal-hotel.fr, hotelcardinal.rouen@wanadoo.fr).

$ Hôtel Le Vieux Carré** is an adorable 13-room place a block from the Museum of Fine Arts. You're greeted by a leafy, half-timbered courtyard, a cozy lobby, and welcoming owners. Rooms are a little tight (mostly double beds) but clean and traditional with floral wallpaper (34 Rue Ganterie, tel. 02 35 71 67 70, www.hotel-vieux-carre.com, vieuxcarre.rouen@gmail.com).

$ Hôtel Morand** is a time-warp place with an Old World hunting-lodge feel and simple but good rooms at fair rates (1 Rue Morland, tel. 02 35 71 46 07, www.morandhotel.com, contact@morandhotel.com).

Near Rouen: To sleep peacefully within a 20-minute drive of town, consider sleepy St-Martin-de-Boscherville, where you can stay at **$ Chambres d'Hôtes Les Hostises de Boscherville.** Christel has four tasteful and spacious rooms, a big garden, and point-blank views to the abbey church—and is the only game in town when it comes to dinner (includes breakfast, book ahead for her cheap-and-tasty €16 "light" dinner of salad, killer quiche, cheese, dessert, and wine, 1 Route de Quevillon, 76840 St-Martin-de-Boscherville, tel. 02 35 34 19 81, www.chambrehôtenormandie.com, hostises.boscherville@gmail.com).

Eating in Rouen

To find the best eating action, prowl the streets between the St. Maclou and St. Ouen churches (Rues Martainville and Damiette) for *crêperies,* wine bars, international cuisine, and traditional restaurants. This is Rouen's liveliest area at night (except Sunday and Monday, when many places are closed).

$$$$ Restaurant La Couronne is a venerable and cozy place to dine very well. Reserve ahead to experience the same cuisine that Julia Child tasted when she ate her first French meal here in 1948 (31 Place du Vieux Marché, tel. 02 35 71 40 90, www.lacouronne. com.fr).

$ Crêperie le St. Romain, between the cathedral and St. Maclou Church, is an excellent budget option. Gentle Mr. Pegis serves filling crêpes with small salads in a warm setting (tables in the rear are best). The hearty *gatiflette*—a crêpe with scalloped potatoes—is delicious (lunch Tue-Sat, dinner Thu-Sat, 52 Rue St. Romain, tel. 02 35 88 90 36).

$$ Dame Cakes is ideal if it's lunchtime or teatime and you need a Jane Austen fix. The decor is from a more precious era, and the baked goods are out of this world. Locals adore the tables in the back garden, while tourists eat up the cathedral view from the first-floor room (garden terrace in back, Mon-Sat 10:30-19:00, closed Sun, 70 Rue St. Romain, tel. 02 35 07 49 31). For more on the history of this place, see page 20.

$ Au P'it Verdot is a lively wine bar-café where locals gather for a glass of wine and meat-and-cheese plates in the thick of restaurant row (appetizers only, Tue-Sat 18:00-24:00, closed Sun-Mon, 13 Rue Père Adam, tel. 02 35 36 34 43).

$ Bistro Nova is a nifty place to eat well in a warm, friendly setting at good prices. The menu changes daily, but one meat, one fish, and one veggie *plat* are always available (excellent wine list, lunch and dinner, closed Sun-Mon, 2 Place du Lieutenant Aubert, tel. 02 35 70 20 25).

$$ La Petite Auberge, a block off Rue Damiette, is the most traditional place I list. It has an Old World interior, a nice terrace, and good prices—and it's open Sundays (good escargot and *entrecôte* with Camembert, reservations smart, closed Mon, 164 Rue Martainville, tel. 02 35 70 80 18).

Rouen Connections

Rouen is well served by trains from Paris and Caen, making Bayeux and the D-Day beaches a snap to reach.

From Rouen by Train to: Paris' Gare St. Lazare (nearly hourly, 1.5 hours), **Bayeux** (14/day, 2.5 hours, change in Caen), **Caen** (14/day, 1.5 hours), **Pontorson/Mont St-Michel** (2/day, 5-7 hours, change in Caen; more with change in Paris, 7 hours).

By Train and Bus to: Honfleur (6/day Mon-Sat, 3/day Sun, 1-hour train to Le Havre, then find Bay D at bus station just outside train station for 30-minute bus trip over Normandy Bridge to Honfleur).

Route Tips for Drivers: Those continuing to Honfleur or the D-Day beaches should consider the Route of the Ancient Abbeys, outlined on page 24.

Honfleur

Gazing at its cozy harbor lined with skinny, soaring houses, it's easy to overlook the historic importance of Honfleur (ohn-flur). For more than a thousand years, sail-ors have enjoyed this port's ideal lo-cation, where the Seine River greets the English Channel. William the Conqueror received supplies shipped from Honfleur. Samuel de Cham-plain sailed from here in 1603 to North America, where he founded Quebec City. The town was also a favorite of 19th-century Impression-

ists who were captivated by Honfleur's unusual light—the result of its river-meets-sea setting. The 19th-century artist Eugène Boudin lived and painted in Honfleur, attracting Monet and other creative types from Paris. In some ways, modern art was born in the fine light of idyllic little Honfleur.

Honfleur escaped the bombs of World War II, and today offers a romantic port enclosed on three sides by sprawling outdoor cafés. Long eclipsed by the gargantuan port of Le Havre just across the Seine, Honfleur happily uses its past as a bar stool...and sits on it.

Orientation to Honfleur

Honfleur is popular—expect crowds on weekends and during sum-mer. All of Honfleur's appealing lanes and activities are within a short stroll of its old port, the Vieux Bassin. The Seine River flows just east of the center, the hills of the Côte de Grâce form its west-ern limit, and Rue de la République slices north-south through the center to the port. Honfleur has two can't-miss sights—the har-bor and St. Catherine Church—and a handful of other intriguing monuments. But really, the town itself is its best sight.

TOURIST INFORMATION

The TI is in the glassy public library *(Mediathéque)* on Quai le Paul-mier, two blocks from the Vieux Bassin (Mon-Sat 9:30-19:00, Sun 10:00-17:00; Sept-June Mon-Sat until 18:30 and closed daily for lunch 12:30-14:00; closed Sun afternoon Nov-Easter; free WCs, tel. 02 31 89 23 30, www.ot-honfleur.fr). Here you can rent a €5 audioguide for a self-guided town walk, pick up regional bus and train schedules, and get information on the D-Day beaches.

ARRIVAL IN HONFLEUR

By Bus: Get off at the small bus station *(gare routière)*, and confirm your departure at the information counter. To reach the TI and old town, turn right as you exit the station and walk five minutes up Quai le Paulmier. Note that the bus stop on Rue de la République is closer to some accommodations (see map on page 30).

By Car: Follow *Centre-Ville* signs, then find your hotel and unload your bags (double-parking is OK for a few minutes). Parking is a headache in Honfleur, especially on summer and holiday weekends. Some hotels offer pay parking; otherwise, your hotelier knows where you can park for free. If you don't mind paying for convenience, Parking du Bassin across from the TI is central (€3/hour, €22/24 hours) or across the short causeway to Parking du Môle (€6/day). Free parking is available farther out at the Naturospace Museum (15-minute walk up Boulevard Charles V, near the beach) and Parking Beaulieu (take Rue St-Nichol to Rue Guillaume de Beaulieu). Street parking, metered during the day, is free from 20:00 to 8:00. See the map on page 30 for parking locations.

HELPFUL HINTS

Museum Pass: The €11-13 museum pass, sold at participating museums, covers the Eugène Boudin Museum, Maisons Satie, and the Museum of Ethnography and Norman Popular Arts (www.musees-honfleur.fr).

Market Day: The area around St. Catherine Church becomes a colorful open-air market every Saturday (9:00-13:00). A smaller organic-food-only market takes place here on Wednesday mornings, and a flea market takes center stage here the first Sunday of every month and also on Wednesday evenings in summer.

Grocery Store: There's one with long hours near the TI (daily July-Aug, closed Mon off-season, 16 Quai le Paulmier).

Regional Products with Panache: Visit **Produits Regionaux Gribouille** for any Norman delicacy you can dream up. Ask about tastings (16 Rue de l'Homme de Bois, tel. 02 31 89 29 54).

Wi-Fi: Free Wi-Fi is available on the port and at several cafés, including the recommended **L'Albatross** and **Le Perroquet Vert.**

Laundry: Lavomatique is a block behind the TI, toward the port (self-service only, daily 7:30-21:30, 4 Rue Notre-Dame). **La Lavandière** has handy drop-off service (Tue-Fri 7:45-12:30 & 14:00-19:00, Sat 7:45-17:00, closed Sun-Mon, two blocks from the harbor at 41 Rue de la République).

Taxi: Call mobile 06 08 60 17 98.

Tourist Train: Honfleur's *petit train* toots you up the Côte de Grâce—the hill overlooking town—and back in about 45

NORMANDY

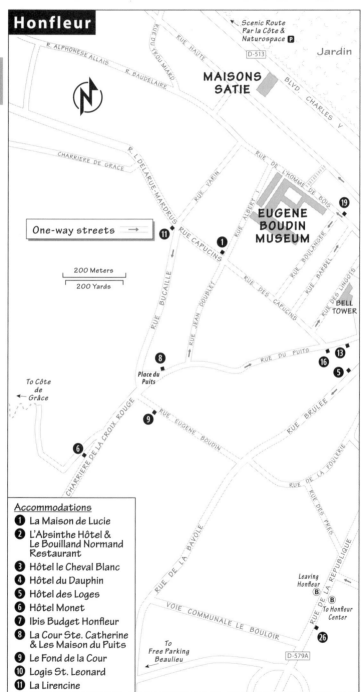

Honfleur

Scenic Route
Par la Côte &
Naturospace P

Jardin

D-513

**MAISONS
SATIE**

BLVD. CHARLES V

R. ALPHONESE ALLAIS

RUE DU TROU MIARD

RUE HAUTE

R. BAUDELAIRE

CHARRIERE DE GRACE

R. L. DELARUE-MARDRUS

RUE VARIN

RUE DE L'HOMME DE BOIS

**EUGENE
BOUDIN
MUSEUM**

RUE ALBERT I

19

One-way streets →

11

RUE CAPUCINS

1

RUE BOULANGER

RUE BARBEL

200 Meters

200 Yards

RUE DES CAPUCINS

RUE DES LINGOTS

**BELL
TOWER**

RUE BUCAILLE

RUE JEAN DOUBLET

8

RUE DU PUITS

16   13

*Place du
Puits*

5

To Côte
de
← Grâce

CHARRIERE DE LA CROIX ROUGE

9   RUE EUGENE BOUDIN

RUE BRULEE

6

RUE DE LA FOULERIE

RUE DES PSES

RUE DE LA BAVOLE

*Leaving
Honfleur*
B   B
To Honfleur
Center

VOIE COMMUNALE LE BOULOIR

RUE DE LA REPUBLIQUE

26

*To
Free Parking
Beaulieu*

D-579A

Accommodations

1 La Maison de Lucie
2 L'Absinthe Hôtel &
  Le Bouilland Normand
  Restaurant
3 Hôtel le Cheval Blanc
4 Hôtel du Dauphin
5 Hôtel des Loges
6 Hôtel Monet
7 Ibis Budget Honfleur
8 La Cour Ste. Catherine
  & Les Maison du Puits
9 Le Fond de la Cour
10 Logis St. Leonard
11 La Lirencine

NORMANDY

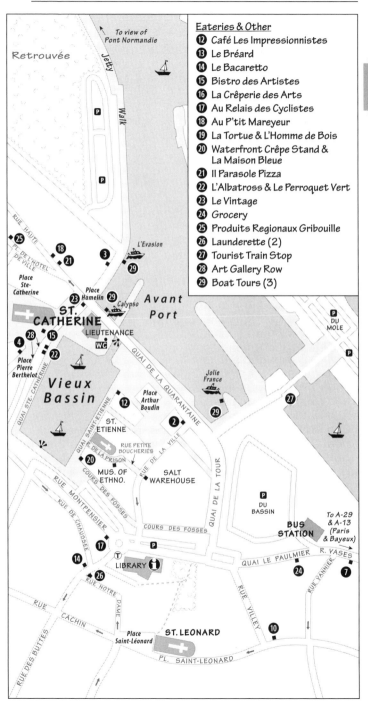

Eateries & Other

12 Café Les Impressionnistes
13 Le Bréard
14 Le Bacaretto
15 Bistro des Artistes
16 La Crêperie des Arts
17 Au Relais des Cyclistes
18 Au P'tit Mareyeur
19 La Tortue & L'Homme de Bois
20 Waterfront Crêpe Stand & La Maison Bleue
21 Il Parasole Pizza
22 L'Albatross & Le Perroquet Vert
23 Le Vintage
24 Grocery
25 Produits Regionaux Gribouille
26 Launderette (2)
27 Tourist Train Stop
28 Art Gallery Row
29 Boat Tours (3)

NORMANDY

minutes (€7, June-Sept daily 10:30-17:30, off-season weekends only, departures on the hour except at lunchtime, leaves from across gray swivel bridge that leads to Parking du Môle).

Sights in Honfleur

▲▲Vieux Bassin (Old Port)

Stand near the water facing Honfleur's square harbor, with the merry-go-round across the lock to your left, and survey the town.

The word "Honfleur" is Scandinavian, meaning the shelter *(fleur)* of Hon (a Viking warlord). This town has been sheltering residents for about a thousand years. During the Hundred Years' War (14th century), the entire harbor was fortified by a big wall with twin gatehouses (the one surviving gatehouse, La Lieutenance, is on your right). A narrow channel allowing boats to pass was protected by a heavy chain.

After the walls were demolished around 1700, those skinny houses on the right side were built for the town's fishermen. How about a room on the top floor, with no elevator? Imagine moving a piano or a refrigerator into one of these units today. The spire halfway up the left side of the port belongs to Honfleur's oldest church. The port, once crammed with fishing boats, now harbors sleek sailboats.

Walk toward the Lieutenance gatehouse. In front of the barrel-vaulted arch (once the entry to the town), you can see a bronze bust of Samuel de Champlain—the explorer who, 400 years ago, sailed with an Honfleur crew—famous for their maritime skills—to make his discoveries in the New World. Champlain is acknowledged as the founder of the Canadian city of Quebec—which remains French-speaking to this day.

Turn around to see various tour and fishing boats and the masts of the high-flying Normandy Bridge (described later) in the distance. Fisherfolk catch flatfish, scallops, and tiny shrimp daily to bring to the Marché au Poisson, located 100 yards to your right (look for white metal structures with blue lettering). Thursday through Sunday, you may see fishermen's wives selling *crevettes* (shrimp). You can buy them *cuites* (cooked) or *vivantes* (alive and wiggly). They are happy to let you sample one (rip off the cute little head and tail, and pop what's left into your mouth—*délicieuse!*), or buy a cupful to go for a few euros.

You'll probably see artists sitting at easels around the harbor, as Boudin and Monet did. Many consider Honfleur the birthplace of 19th-century Impressionism. This was a time when people began to revere the out-of-doors, and pretty towns like Honfleur and the nearby coast made perfect subjects (and still are), thanks to the unusual luminosity of the region. And with the advent of new railway lines in the late 1800s, artists could travel to the best light like never before. Monet came here to visit the artist Boudin, a hometown boy, and the battle cry of the Impressionists—"Out of the studio and into the light!"—was born. Artists set up their easels along the harbor to catch the light playing on the line of buildings, slate shingles, timbers, geraniums, clouds, and reflections in the water—much as they still do today.

If you're an early riser, you can watch what's left of Honfleur's fishing fleet prepare for the day, and you just might experience that famous luminosity.

Old Honfleur

A chance to study the Lego-style timber-frame houses of Honfleur awaits just off the harbor. On the southern quay, next to the Church of St. Etienne, head up Rue de la Prison (past the worthwhile Museum of Ethnography; see page 37) and bend around to Rue des Petites Boucheries for some prime examples. The beams of these buildings were numbered so they could be disassembled and moved. Walking through a slate-sided passage, you'll pop out onto Rue de la Ville with more historic Norman architecture. Across the way is one of three huge 17th-century salt warehouses. It's worth entering (often €1) to see the huge stone hall with its remarkable wooden ceiling and imagine the importance of salt as a preservative before refrigeration existed.

Strategically positioned Honfleur guarded Paris from a naval attack up the Seine. That's why the king fortified it with a wall in the 1300s. In the 1600s, when England was no longer a threat, the walls were torn down, leaving the town with some wide boulevards (like the one in front of the TI) and plenty of stones (like those that made the salt warehouse).

▲▲St. Catherine Church (Eglise Ste. Catherine)

St. Catherine's replaced an earlier stone church, destroyed in the Hundred Years' War. In those chaotic times, the town's money was spent to fortify its walls, leaving only enough funds to erect a wooden church. The unusual wood-shingled exterior suggests that this church has a different story to tell than most. In the last months of World War II, a bomb fell through the church's roof—

but didn't explode—leaving this unique church intact for you to visit today.

Cost and Hours: Free, daily 9:00-18:30, Sept-June until 17:15, Place Ste-Catherine.

Visiting the Church: Walk inside. You'd swear that if it were turned over, the building would float—the legacy of a community of sailors and fishermen, with loads of talented boat-builders (and no church architect). When workers put up the first (left) nave in 1466, it soon became apparent that more space was needed—so a second was built in 1497 (on the right). Because it felt too much like a market hall, they added side aisles.

The oak columns were prepared as if the wood was meant for a ship—soaked in seawater for seven years and then dried for seven years. Notice some pillars are full-length and others are supported by stone bases. Trees come in different sizes, yet each pillar had to be the same length.

The pipe organ (from 1772, rebuilt in 1953) behind you is popular for concerts, and half of the modern pews are designed to flip so that you can face the music. Take a close look at the balustrade (below the organ) with carved wooden panels featuring 17 musical instruments used in the 16th century.

Find a seat, and enjoy the worshipful ambience of this beautiful space. But don't sit in the box in the center; this was reserved for the local noble lord and his family. If you want to gossip, head to the "cackling zone"—an open-air narthex (outside, about halfway up on the right) where historically (and perhaps hysterically) people gathered after Mass.

Bell Tower: The church's bell tower was built away from the church to avoid placing too much stress on the wooden church's roof, and to help minimize fire hazards. Notice the funky shingled chestnut beams that run from its squat base to support the skinny tower, and find the small, faded wooden sculpture of a tiny St. Catherine over the door. Until recently the bell ringer lived in the bell tower.

HONFLEUR'S MUSEUMS AND GALLERIES

Eugène Boudin established Honfleur's artistic tradition. The town remains a popular haunt for artists, many of whom display their works in Honfleur's many art galleries (the best ones are along the streets between St. Catherine Church and the port). As you stroll around the town taking in its old sights, take time to enjoy today's art, too.

▲Eugène Boudin Museum

This pleasing little museum opened in 1869 and has several interesting floors with many paintings of Honfleur and the surrounding countryside, giving you a feel for Honfleur in the 1800s. (The museum was recently renovated, so expect some changes from this description.)

NORMANDY

Cost and Hours: €8 in summer, €6 off-season, covered by museum pass; Wed-Mon 10:00-12:00 & 14:00-18:00, closed Tue, shorter hours Oct-April; audioguide-€2 (good but skippable), elevator, Rue de l'Homme de Bois, tel. 02 31 89 54 00, www.musees-honfleur.fr.

Visiting the Museum: Pick up a map at the ticket counter, tip your beret to Eugène Boudin, and climb the stairs (or take the elevator). The first floor has good WCs and kids' activity rooms.

Second Floor: Making a right off the stairs leads you into a large room of appealing 20th-century paintings and sculpture created by artists while living in Honfleur (special exhibits sometimes occupy this space). A left off the stairs leads through a room of temporary exhibits to the *Peintures du 19eme Siècle* room, a small gallery of 19th-century paintings. Focus your time here. Boudin's artwork is shown alongside that of his colleagues and contemporaries (usually Claude Monet and Gustave Courbet), letting you see how those masters took Boudin's approach to the next level. Boudin loved his outdoor world and filled his paintings with port scenes, the sea, and big skies. Find the glass display case in the rear titled *Précurseur de l'Impressionisme*, with little pastel drawings, and follow Boudin's art chronologically, as it evolves.

When Boudin and other Honfleur artists showed their work in Paris, they created enough of a stir that Normandy came into vogue. Many Parisian artists (including Monet and other early Impressionists) traveled to Honfleur to dial in to the action. Boudin himself made a big impression on the father of Impressionism by introducing Monet to the practice of painting outside. This collection of Boudin's paintings—which the artist gave to his hometown—shows how his technique developed, from realistic portrayals of subjects (outlines colored in, like a coloring book) to masses of colors catching light (Impressionism). Boudin's beach scenes at the end of the room, showing aristocrats taking a healthy saltwater dip, helped fuel that style. His skies were good enough to earn him the nickname "King of Skies."

Third Floor: Follow the steps that lead up from the Boudin room to the small, enjoyable Hambourg/Rachet collection, which is largely from the mid-20th century. Don't miss the smashing painting of Honfleur at twilight. Also on the third floor is a worthwhile collection of 20th-century works by artists who lived and learned in Honfleur, including the Fauvist painter Raoul Dufy and Yves Brayer. There's an exceptional view of the Normandy Bridge through the big windows.

NORMANDY

Eugène Boudin (1824-1898)

Born in Honfleur, Boudin was the son of a harbor pilot. As an amateur teenage artist, he found work in an art-supply store that catered to famous artists from Paris (such as landscapists Corot and Millet) who came to paint the seaside. Boudin himself studied in Paris and his work was exhibited there, but he kept his hometown roots.

At age 30 Boudin met the teenage Claude Monet. Monet had grown up in nearby Le Havre and, like Boudin, sketched the world around him—beaches, boats, and small-town life. Boudin encouraged him to don a scarf, set up his easel outdoors, and paint the scene exactly as he saw it. Today, we say: "Well, duh!" But "open-air" painting was unorthodox for artists trained to thoroughly study their subjects in the perfect lighting of a controlled studio setting. Boudin didn't teach Monet as much as give him the courage to follow his artistic instincts.

In the 1860s and 1870s, Boudin spent summers at his farm (St. Siméon) on the outskirts of Honfleur, hosting Monet, Edouard Manet, and other hangers-on. They taught Boudin the Impressionist techniques of using bright colors and building a subject with many individual brushstrokes. Boudin adapted those "strokes" to build subjects with "patches" of color. In 1874, Boudin joined the renegade Impressionists at their "revolutionary" exhibition in Paris.

▲Maisons Satie

If Honfleur is over-the-top cute, this museum, housed in composer Erik Satie's birthplace, is a burst of witty charm—just like the musical genius it honors. If you like Satie's music, this is a delight—a 1920s "Yellow Submarine." If not, it can be a ho-hum experience. Allow an hour for your visit.

Cost and Hours: €6.30, includes audioguide, covered by museum pass; May-Sept Wed-Mon 10:00-19:00, off-season 11:00-18:00, closed Jan-mid-Feb and Tue year-round; last entry one hour before closing, 5-minute walk from harbor at 67 Boulevard Charles V, tel. 02 31 89 11 11, www.musees-honfleur.fr.

Visiting the Museum: As you wander from room to room with your included audioguide, infrared signals transmit bits of Satie's dreamy music, along with a first-person story. As if you're living as an artist in 1920s Paris, you'll drift through a weird and whimsical series of old-school installations—winged pears, strangers in windows, and small girls with green eyes. The finale—performed by you—is the *Laboratory of Emotions* pedal-go-round, a self-propelled carousel where your feet create the music (pedal softly). For a relaxing finale, enjoy the 12-minute movie (plays by request, French only) featuring modern dance springing from *Parade,* Satie's collaboration with Pablo Picasso and Jean Cocteau. You'll even hear the boos and whistles that greeted these ballets' debuts.

▲Museum of Ethnography and Norman Popular Arts (Musée d'Ethnographie et d'Art Populaire Normand)

Honfleur's engaging little Museum of Ethnography and Norman Popular Arts (pick up English translation at the desk) is located in the old prison and courthouse a short block off the harbor in the heart of Old Honfleur. It re-creates typical rooms from Honfleur's past and crams them with objects of daily life—costumes, furniture, looms, and an antique printing press. You'll see the old yard and climb through two stories of furnished rooms. The museum paints a picture of daily life in Honfleur during the time when its ships were king and the city had global significance. (Skip the adjacent Museum of the Sea.)

Cost and Hours: €4.20, Tue-Sun 10:00-12:00 & 14:00-18:30, shorter hours off-season, closed mid-Nov-mid-Feb and Mon year-round, Rue de la Prison, www.musees-honfleur.fr.

HONFLEUR WALKS AND DRIVES
▲Côte de Grâce Walk (or Drive)

For good exercise and a bird's-eye view of Honfleur and the Normandy Bridge, go for an uphill 30-minute walk (or quick drive) up to the Côte de Grâce—best in the early morning, late afternoon, or at sunset. From St. Catherine Church, **walk** up Rue du Puits and then follow the blue-on-white *Rampe du Mont Joli* signs to reach the splendid view over Honfleur and the Normandy Bridge at the top. This viewpoint alone justifies the climb.

Drivers should head up Rue Brulée and make a right on Rue Eugène Boudin), then take a hard left at Rue de Puits and follow *Côte de Grâce* signs.

At the top, walkers and drivers can continue past the viewpoint for about 300 yards along a country lane to the **Chapel of Notre-Dame de Grâce,** built in the early 1600s by the mariners and people of Honfleur (open daily 8:30-17:30). Model boats hang from the ceiling, pictures of boats balance high on the walls, and several stained-glass windows are decorated with images of sailors at sea praying to the Virgin Mary. Find the 23 church bells hanging on a wood rack 20 steps to the right as you leave the church and imagine the racket they make (the bells ring four times an hour). Below the chapel, a lookout offers a sweeping view of super-industrial Le Havre and the Seine estuary where the river hits the Manche (English Channel).

Jetty/Park Walk

Take a level stroll in Honfleur along the water past the Hôtel le Cheval Blanc to find the mouth of the Seine River and big ships at sea. You'll pass kid-friendly parks carpeted with flowers and grass, and continue past the lock connecting Honfleur to the Seine and the sea. Grand and breezy vistas of the sea and smashing views of the Normandy Bridge reward the diligent walker (allow 20 minutes to reach the best views).

NEAR HONFLEUR

Boat Excursions

Boat trips in and around Honfleur depart from various docks between Hôtel le Cheval Blanc and the opposite end of the outer port (Easter-Oct usually about 11:00-17:00). The tour boat *Calypso* takes good 45-minute spins around Honfleur's harbor (€6, mobile 06 71 64 50 46, Jetée de la Lieutenance). Other cruises run to the Normandy Bridge, which, unfortunately, means two boring trips through the locks (€11/1.5 hours, choose between *Jolie France*, near Parking du Môle, mobile 06 71 64 50 46, www.promenade-en-bateau-honfleur.fr, Jetée du Transit; or *L'Evasion* near Hôtel le Cheval Blanc, mobile 06 31 89 21 10, Quai des Passagers).

Normandy Bridge (Pont de Normandie)

The 1.25-mile-long Normandy Bridge is the longest cable-stayed bridge in the Western world (€6 toll each way, not worth a detour). This is a key piece of European expressway that links the Atlantic ports from Belgium to Spain. View the bridge from Honfleur (better from an excursion boat or the Jetty Walk described earlier, and best at night, when bridge is floodlit). Also consider visiting the bridge's free Exhibition Hall (just before tollbooth on Le Havre side, daily 8:00-19:00). The Seine finishes its winding journey here, dropping only 1,500 feet from its source, 450 miles away. The river flows so slowly that, in certain places, a stiff breeze can send it flowing upstream.

▲Etrétat

France's answer to the White Cliffs of Dover, these chalky cliffs soar high above a calm, crescent beach. Walking trails lead hikers from the small seaside resort of Etrétat along a vertiginous route with sensational views (and crowds of hikers in summer and on weekends). You'll recognize these cliffs—and the arches and stone spire that decorate them—from countless Impressionist paintings, including several at the Eugène Boudin Museum in Honfleur. The small, Coney Island-like town holds plenty of cafés and a TI (Place Maurice Guillard, tel. 02 35 27 05 21, www.etretat.net).

Getting There: Etrétat is north of Le Havre. To get here by car (50 minutes), cross the Normandy Bridge and follow A-29, then exit at *sortie Etrétat.* Buses serve Etrétat from Le Havre's *gare routière,* adjacent to the train station (5/day, 1 hour, www.keolis-seine-maritime.com).

Sleeping in Etrétat: $$$$ Dormy House has a brilliant setting and makes a nice splurge for a room and/or restaurant with a view (Route du Havre at the edge of Etrétat, tel. 02 35 27 07 88, www.dormy-house.com, info@etretat-hotel.com).

Sleeping in Honfleur

Though Honfleur is popular in summer, it's busiest on weekends and holidays (blame Paris). English is widely spoken (blame vacationing Brits). A few moderate accommodations remain, but most hotels are pretty pricey. Only two hotels have elevators (Hôtel le Cheval Blanc and Ibis Budget Honfleur), but Hotel Monet has ground-floor rooms.

HOTELS

$$$$ La Maison de Lucie*** is a fine *Normand* splurge and greets its guests with a garden courtyard, sumptuous lounges, and antique-filled rooms (suites available, 44 Rue des Capucines, tel. 02 31 49 41, www.lamaisondelucie.com, info@lamaisondelucie.com).

$$$ L'Absinthe Hôtel*** offers 11 tastefully restored rooms with king-size beds in two locations. The older rooms in the main (reception) section come with wood-beamed decor and share a cozy public lounge with a fireplace). Six rooms are located above their next-door restaurant and have views of the modern port and three-star, state-of-the-art comfort (includes breakfast, air-con in both buildings, private pay parking, 1 Rue de la Ville, tel. 02 31 89 23 23, www.absinthe.fr, reservation@absinthe.fr).

$$$ Hôtel le Cheval Blanc*** is a waterfront splurge with port views from all of its 35 plush and pricey rooms (many with queen beds), plus a rare-in-this-town elevator and a spa, but no air-conditioning—noise can be a problem with windows open (family rooms, pay parking, 2 Quai des Passagers, tel. 02 31 81 65 00, www.hotel-honfleur.com, info@hotel-honfleur.com).

$$ Hôtel du Dauphin,*** wrapped in a half-timbered shell, is ideally located, with narrow stairs (normal in Honfleur) and an Escher-esque floor plan. The 30 standard rooms (in two buildings) are an acceptable value, (Wi-Fi in main building only, a stone's throw from St. Catherine Church at 10 Place Pierre Berthelot, tel. 02 31 89 15 53, www.hoteldudauphin.com, info@hotelhonfleur.com).

com). The same owners also run the **$$ Hôtel des Loges***** a few doors up, with larger rooms. Both hotels offer discounts for Rick Steves readers in 2018—ask for details when you reserve.

$$ Hôtel Monet,** on the road to the Côte de Grâce and a 15-minute walk down to the port, is a good value, particularly for drivers. This tranquil spot offers 16 comfortable rooms, all with private patios that surround a gravel parking area (family rooms, free and easy parking, Charrière du Puits, tel. 02 31 89 00 90, www.hotel-monet-honfleur.com, contact@hotel-monet-honfleur.com). Reception is closed 13:00-17:00.

$ Ibis Budget Honfleur is modern, efficient, trim, and cheap, with prefab bathrooms and an antiseptically clean ambience (family rooms, reception closed 21:00-6:00 but automatic check-in with credit card available 24 hours, elevator, across from bus station and main parking lot on Rue des Vases, tel. 08 92 68 07 81, www.ibisbudget.com, h2716-re@accor.com).

CHAMBRES D'HOTES

The TI has a long list of Honfleur's many *chambres d'hôtes* (rooms in private homes), but most are too far from the town center. Those listed here are good values.

$$ La Cour Ste. Catherine is an enchanting bed-and-breakfast run by the cheery and open-hearted Madame Giaglis ("call me Liliane"). Her six big, tasteful rooms—each with a separate sitting area—surround a perfectly Norman courtyard with a small terrace, fine plantings, and a cozy lounge area ideal for cool evenings (includes good breakfast, small apartments and cottage with kitchen available, cash only, ask about free parking when you book, 200 yards up Rue du Puits from St. Catherine Church at #74, tel. 02 31 89 42 40, www.coursaintecatherine.com, coursaintecatherine@orange.fr).

$$ Le Fond de la Cour, kitty-corner to Le Cour St. Catherine and run by British expats Amanda and Craig, offers a good mix of crisp, modern, and comfortable accommodations around a peaceful courtyard. There's a large cottage that can sleep four, a good room for families, and four comfortable doubles (non-cottage rooms include English-style breakfast, free street parking, limited private pay parking, 29 Rue Eugène Boudin, mobile 06 72 20 72 98, www.lefonddelacour.com, amanda.ferguson@orange.fr).

$$ Les Maisons du Puits is an assembly of several small "apartments" for 2-4 people, all centrally situated and reasonably priced

(14 Rue du Puits, mobile 06 03 98 64 91, www.lesmaisonsdupuits. com, lesmaisonsdupuits@gmail.com).

$$ Logis St. Leonard is a sweet three-room place where guests are given the run of the house (well, almost). Overseen by earnest Anne-Marie, it is decorated with oodles of personal touches and has a fine garden (cash only, includes breakfast, mobile 06 63 72 72 38, annemariecarneiro14@gmail.com).

$ La Lirencine is central and a good value, with three quite comfortable rooms with kitchenettes and a shared terrace. Charming Annick Proffit is your host (cash only, 3 Rue Lucie Delarue Mardrus, mobile 06 70 70 98 65, www.chambrecharmehonfleur. com, chambrecharmehonfleur14@gmail.com).

NORMANDY

Eating in Honfleur

Eat seafood, crêpes, or cream sauces here. Choose between an irresistible waterfront table at one of the many lookalike places lining the harbor, or finer dining elsewhere in town. It's best to call ahead to reserve (particularly on weekends).

DINING ALONG THE HARBOR

Survey the eateries lining the harbor (all open Wed when other places are closed). The food isn't great, but you'll find plenty of salads, crêpes, and seafood—and a great setting. Heaters and canopies make dining outdoors a good option even in chilly weather. On a languid evening, it's hard to pass up. Even if you dine elsewhere, come to the harbor for a before- or after-dinner drink. **Café Les Impressionnistes** and **La Maison Bleue,** on the Quai St. Etienne side of the harbor, own the best views of Honfleur.

BETTER FOOD, NO VIEWS

While I wouldn't blame you for enjoying a forgettable meal in an unforgettable setting on the harborfront, consider these finer alternatives a couple blocks away.

$$$$ Le Bréard is a fine place to dial it up a little and eat very well for a fair price. The decor is low key but elegant, the cuisine is inventive, delicious, and not particularly *Normand,* and the service is excellent (closed Mon, 7 Rue du Puits, tel. 02 31 89 53 40).

$$ Le Bouilland Normand hides a block off the port on a pleasing square and offers true *Normand* cuisine at reasonable prices. Annette, Claire, and chef-hubby Bruno provide quality dishes and enjoy serving travelers (closed Wed and Sun, dine inside or out, 7 Rue de la Ville, tel. 02 31 89 02 41).

$ Le Bacaretto wine bar-café is run by laid-back Hervé, the antithesis of a wine snob. This relaxed, tiny, wine-soaked place offers a fine selection of well-priced wines by the glass and a small but appealing assortment of appetizers and *plats du jour* that can make a full meal (closed Wed-Thu for lunch and Sun for dinner, 44 Rue de la Chaussée, tel. 02 31 14 83 11).

$$ Bistro des Artistes is a two-woman operation with a pleasant 10-table dining room (call ahead for a window table). Hardworking Anne-Marie cooks up huge portions; one course is plenty...and maybe a dessert (great salads, closed Wed, 30 Place Berthelot, tel. 02 31 89 95 90).

$ La Crêperie des Arts serves up crêpes in a comfortable setting with a huge fireplace, and is a good, centrally located budget option (13 Rue du Puits, tel. 02 31 89 14 02).

$ Au Relais des Cyclistes, on a busy street near the TI, is an eclectic, lively, pub-like place for a simple, inexpensive meal with fun indoor and outdoor seating (closed Thu, 10 Place de la Porte de Rouen, tel. 02 31 89 09 76).

$$$ Au P'tit Mareyeur is whisper-formal, intimate, all about seafood, and a good value. The ground floor and upstairs rooms offer equal comfort and ambience (famous €38 Bouillabaisse Honfleuraise, closed Tue-Wed and Jan, 4 Rue Haute, tel. 02 31 98 84 23, Julie speaks some English).

At **$$ La Tortue,** the owner/chef prepares tasty cuisine, including good vegetarian dishes, and serves it in a pleasing setting (open daily in summer, closed Tue-Wed rest of year, tel. 02 31 81 24 60, 36 Rue de l'Homme de Bois).

$$ L'Homme de Bois combines cozy ambience with authentic *Normand* cuisine that is loved by locals, so book a day ahead. Fish is their forte (daily, a few outside tables, skip the upstairs room, 30 Rue de l'Homme de Bois, tel. 02 31 89 75 27).

Breakfast: If it's even close to sunny, skip your hotel breakfast and eat on the port, where several cafés offer *petit déjeuner* (€4-7 for continental fare, €7-14 for more elaborate choices—the Bagel Burger at **L'Albatross** is filling). Morning sun and views are best from the high side of the harbor.

Dessert: Honfleur is ice-cream crazy, with gelato and traditional ice-cream shops on every corner. If you need a Ben & Jerry's ice-cream fix or a scrumptious dessert crêpe, find the **waterfront stand** at the southeast corner of the Vieux Bassin.

Nighttime Food to Go: Order a pizza to go until late from **$ Il Parasole** (2 Rue Haute, tel. 02 31 98 94 29), and enjoy a picnic dinner with port views a few steps away at the Lieutenant gatehouse.

Nightlife: Nightlife in Honfleur centers on the old port. Several bar/cafés line the high-building side of the port, including these down-and-dirty watering holes: pub-like **L'Albatross** (a fun and smoky clubhouse) and **Le Perroquet Vert** (also cool but more existential—"those lights are so..."). **Le Vintage,** just off the port, has live piano and jazz on weekend nights (closed Tue, 8 Quai des Passagers, tel. 02 31 89 05 28).

Honfleur Connections

There's no direct train service to Honfleur, so you must connect by bus or car. The handy, express PrestoBus (line #39) links Honfleur with train service in Caen and Le Havre, but runs only twice a day. Bus #50 runs between Le Havre, Honfleur and Lisieux; the scenic *par la côte* bus #20 connects Le Havre, Honfleur, Deauville, and Caen. Although train and bus service usually are coordinated, confirm your connection with the helpful staff at Honfleur's bus station (English info desk open Mon-Fri 9:30-12:00 & 13:15-18:00, in summer also Sat-Sun, tel. 02 31 89 28 41, www.busverts.fr). If the station is closed, you can get schedules at the TI. Rail-pass holders will save money by connecting through Deauville, as bus fares increase with distance.

From Honfleur by Bus and/or Train to: Caen (express PrestoBus 2/day, 1 hour; bus #20 4/day direct, 2 hours); **Bayeux** (2-3/day, 1.5 hours; first take PrestoBus #39 or bus #20 to Caen, then 20-minute train to Bayeux); **Rouen** (6/day Mon-Sat, 3/day Sun, bus-and-train combo involves 30-minute bus ride over Normandy Bridge to Le Havre, then easy transfer to 1-hour train to Rouen); **Paris'** Gare St. Lazare (13/day, 2-3.5 hours, by bus to Caen, Lisieux, Deauville, or Le Havre, then train to Paris; buses from Honfleur meet most Paris trains).

Route Tips for Drivers: If driving to Rouen, see the Route of the Ancient Abbeys on page 24. If connecting to the D-Day beaches, consider taking the scenic route *"par la côte"* to Trouville, which goes past sea views, thatched hamlets, and stupendous mansions. From Honfleur, drive to the port, pass Hôtel du Cheval Blanc, and stick to this road (D-513) to Trouville, then follow signs for A-13 to Caen.

Bayeux

Only six miles from the D-Day beaches, Bayeux was the first city liberated after the landing on June 6, 1944. Incredibly, the town was spared the bombs of World War II. The Allied Command needed an intact town from which to administer the push to Berlin. And after a local chaplain made sure London knew that his city was neither strategically important nor a German headquarters, a scheduled bombing raid was canceled—making Bayeux the closest city to the D-Day landing site not destroyed. Even without its famous medieval tapestry and proximity to the D-Day beaches, Bayeux would be worth a visit for its enjoyable town center and awe-inspiring cathedral, beautifully illuminated at night. Its location and manageable size (pop. 14,000) make Bayeux an ideal home base for visiting the area's sights, particularly if you lack a car.

Orientation to Bayeux

Bayeux grew up along the Aure River. Its main street (Rue St. Jean) was a Roman road. The river powered the town's waterwheels and flushed its waste as its industry grew. The TI is located in the old fish market over the river, and the nearby waterwheel was part of the tanning and dyeing industry in the 15th century. Across from the Bayeux Tapestry museum, another waterwheel once powered a flour mill (now a recommended crêpe restaurant); its lock created a mill pond which did double-duty as the bishop's fish pond.

TOURIST INFORMATION

The TI is on a small bridge two blocks north of the cathedral. Ask for bus schedules to the beaches and inquire about special events and concerts. They have a good and free D-Day brochure, but World War II buffs may prefer the D-Day map (about €5) showing troop deployments and more (June-Aug Mon-Sat 9:00-19:00, Sun 9:00-13:00 & 14:00-18:00; April-May and Sept-Oct Mon-Sat 9:30-12:30 & 14:00-18:00, Sun 10:00-13:00 & 14:00-18:00; shorter hours off-season; on Pont St. Jean leading to Rue St. Jean, tel. 02 31 51 28 28, www.bessin-normandie.com).

ARRIVAL IN BAYEUX

By Train and Bus: Trains and buses share the same station (bag storage available across from station (see "Helpful Hints," later). It's a 15-minute **walk** from the station to the tapestry, and 15 minutes from the tapestry to Place St. Patrice. To reach the tapestry, the cathedral, and recommended hotels, cross the major street in front of the station and follow Rue de Cremel toward *l'Hôpital*, then turn left on Rue Nesmond. Find signs to the *Tapisserie* (tapestry) or continue on to the cathedral. **Taxis** usually wait at the station—allow €9 to any recommended hotel or sight in Bayeux, and €21 to Arromanches (€32 after 19:00 and on Sundays, taxi tel. 02 31 92 92 40 or mobile 06 70 40 07 96).

By Car: Look for the cathedral spires and follow signs for *Centre-Ville*, and then signs for the *Tapisserie* or your hotel (individual hotels are well-signed from the ring road). Day-trippers will find pay parking lots in the town center (including at the Hôtel de Ville near the TI; and at Place St. Patrice, 3-hour limit, free parking 12:00-14:00 & 19:00-21:00). You can park for free along the ring road near the station and at a few lots in the city (the TI has a map of free parking, or ask your hotelier). Parking areas with blue lines require a cardboard clock displayed on your dashboard (buy at any *tabac*, 3-hour limit).

Drivers connecting Bayeux with Mont St-Michel should use the speedy, free A-84 autoroute (from near the train station, follow signs to *Villars-Bocage,* then A-84).

By Airport Transfer from Paris: It's possible to link Paris and Normandy without driving or connecting by train. **Albion** (run by American Adrienne Sion) organizes transfers between Paris airports and Bayeux (1-3 people-€450, up to 8 people-€600, transfers from central Paris possible, extra for stops en route at Giverny or Honfleur, tel. 02 31 78 88 88, 24-hour calling/texting via WhatsApp: mobile 06 80 28 65 61, www.albion-voyages.com).

HELPFUL HINTS

Market Days: The Saturday open-air market on Place St. Patrice is Bayeux's best, though the Wednesday market on pedestrian Rue St. Jean is pleasant. Both end by 13:00. Don't leave your car on Place St. Patrice on a Friday night, as it will be towed early Saturday.

Grocery Store: Carrefour City, at Rue St. Jean 14, is next to the recommended Hôtel Churchill (long hours Mon-Sat, Sun until 14:00).

Baggage Storage: You can leave bags at the Maison du Vélo bike-rental shop on the ring road, across from the train station (daily 9:00-12:30 & 13:30-18:30 in high season, 43 Boulevard Sadi Carnot).

Laundry: A launderette is a block behind the TI, on Rue Maréchal Foch. Another launderette is near Place St. Patrice, at 69 Rue des Bouchers (both open daily 7:00-21:00).

Bike Rental: These two places rent both electric and standard bikes. **Vélos Location** is across from the TI and delivers to outlying hotels (daily 8:00-20:30, closes earlier off-season, inside grocery store at Impasse de Islet, tel. 02 31 92 89 16, www.velosbayeux.com). **Maison du Vélo** is across from the train station (see "Baggage Storage," earlier).

Taxi: Call 02 31 92 92 40 or mobile 06 70 40 07 96.

Car Rental: Bayeux offers three choices. **Hertz** is the only one that allows you to drop off in a different city (Mon-Fri 8:30-18:00, Sat 9:00-17:00, at the train station, tel. 02 31 16 07 19). **Renault Rent** is just below the train station on the ring road at the Renault dealership (16 Boulevard Sadi Carnot, tel. 02 31 51 18 51). Allow about €50-70/day with a 200-kilometer limit, which is sufficient to see the key sights from Arromanches to Utah Beach—you'll drive about 180 kilometers.

NORMANDY

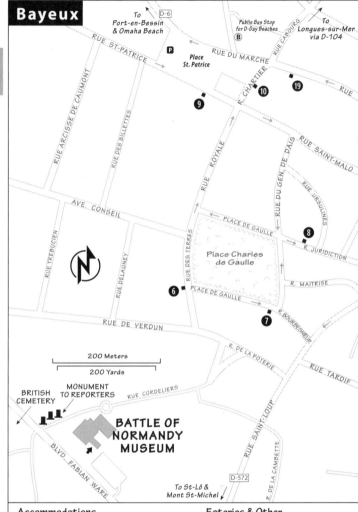

Bayeux

Accommodations

1. Villa Lara
2. Hôtel Churchill & Carrefour City Grocery
3. Hôtel le Lion d'Or
4. Hôtel Reine Mathilde & Le Garde Manger
5. Hôtel au Georges VII & Café
6. Le Petit Matin B&B
7. Logis les Remparts B&B & Calvados
8. Manoir Sainte Victoire
9. Hôtel d'Argouges
10. Hôtel Mogador

Eateries & Other

11. Le Moulin de la Galette
12. La Rapière
13. Le Volet Qui Penche
14. L'Angle Saint Laurent
15. Le Pommier
16. Au P'tit Bistrot
17. La Fringale
18. Bag Storage & Bike Rental
19. Launderette (2)
20. Bayeux Shuttle & Bike Rental
21. Renault Car Rental
22. Hertz Car Rental

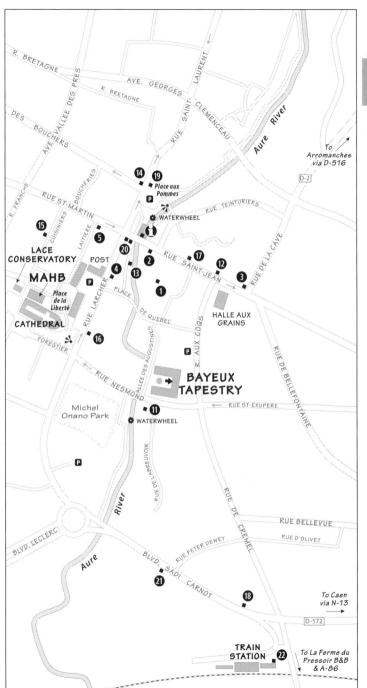

NORMANDY

Bayeux Shuttle rents cars equipped with Wi-Fi (daily 7:45-18:00, across from Bayeux TI at Impasse de Islet, tel. 09 70 44 51 11, bookings@ouilou.com).

Calvados Tasting: For a fun and easy cider sampling, drop by the recommended **Logis les Remparts** B&B (Tue-Sat 10:00-19:00, closed Sun-Mon, 4 Rue Bourbesneur, tel. 02 31 92 50 40).

Tours in Bayeux

Self-Guided Walking Tour: Pick up the map called *Découvrez Vieux Bayeux* at the TI, which corresponds to bronze info plates embedded in sidewalks around town.

Guided Walks of Old Bayeux: For a chatty, anecdote-filled stroll through the historic center—with no interiors but plenty of factoids—join Christèle or Marie-Noëlle for a guided walk (€15, daily April-Sept, 2-hour walk generally at 9:30 and 1.5-hour walk at 17:00, rain or shine, leave from TI, private tours possible year-round, confirm schedule at www.discovery-walks.org).

Bike Tours of Bayeux: Hugo at Petite Reine runs electric bike tours of Bayeux (2 hours-€45) and the D-Day beaches (all day-€75-115, mobile 06 80 87 87 37, https://us.petitereinenormandie.fr/).

Touristy Choo-Choo Train: Bayeux's tourist train leaves hourly from the TI for a 35-minute ride through town with recorded English commentary (€7, pay driver).

Sights in Bayeux

Sightseeing Tips: Bayeux's three main museums—the Bayeux Tapestry, Battle of Normandy Memorial Museum, and MAHB—offer combo-tickets that will save you money if you see more than one sight. Combo-tickets covering two sights cost €12; for all three it's €15 (buy at the first sight you visit). Note that many sights close in January.

▲▲▲Bayeux Tapestry (Tapisserie de Bayeux)

Made of wool embroidered onto linen cloth, this historically precious document is a mesmerizing 70-yard-long cartoon. The tapestry tells the story of William the Conqueror's rise from duke of Normandy to king of England, and shows his victory over England's King Harold at the Battle of Hastings in 1066. Long and skinny, the tapestry was designed to hang in the nave of Bayeux's cathedral as a reminder for locals of their ancestor's courage. The terrific museum that houses the tapestry is an unusually good chance to teach your kids about the Middle Ages. Models, mannequins, a movie, and more make it an engaging, fun place to visit.

Cost and Hours: €9.50, combo-ticket with other Bayeux museums, includes excellent audioguide for adults and special kids' version; daily May-Aug 9:00-19:00, March-April and Sept-Oct until 18:30; Nov-Dec and Feb 9:30-12:30 & 14:00-18:00, closed Jan; last entry 45 minutes before closing; 13 bis Rue de Nesmond, tel. 02 31 51 25 50, www.bayeuxmuseum.com. Photography of the actual tapestry is not allowed, but you can take pictures of a replica.

Planning Your Visit: It's busiest in August, and most crowded from 10:00 to 17:00. Arrive before 10:00, during lunch, or late in the day (lunchtime is most reliably quiet). As audiotours cannot be paused, you are limited to 25 minutes with the tapestry. It's a strict one-way route. Allow at least a full hour for your complete museum visit.

Film: When buying your ticket, get the schedule for the English version of the 16-minute battle film (runs every 40 minutes). Because you can watch the film only after viewing the tapestry, and the last show time is about an hour before closing, arriving late means no film.

Visiting the Museum: Your visit starts with the actual **tapestry,** accompanied by an included audioguide that gives a top-notch, fast-moving, 25-minute scene-by-scene narration complete with period music (no pausing or rewinding—if you lose your place, find

subtitles in Latin). Remember, the tapestry is Norman propaganda: The English (the bad guys, referred to as *les goddamns,* after a phrase the French kept hearing them say) are shown with mustaches and long hair; the French (*les* good guys) are clean-cut and clean-shaven—with even the backs of their heads shaved for a better helmet fit.

Appreciate the fun details—such as the bare legs in scene 4 or Harold's pouting expressions in various frames—and look for references to places you may have visited (like Dinan). Pay strict attention to scene 23, where Harold takes his oath to William; the importance of keeping one's word is the point of the tapestry. Get close and (almost) feel the tapestry's texture.

Next, you'll climb upstairs into a room filled with engaging **exhibits,** including a full-size replica of a Viking ship much like the one William used to cross the Channel (Normans inherited their weaponry and seafaring skills from the Norsemen). You'll also see mannequins (find William looking unmoved with his new crown), a replica of the Domesday Book (an inventory of noble's

The Battle of Hastings

Because of this pivotal battle, the most memorable date of the Middle Ages is 1066. England's king, Edward the Confessor, was about to die without an heir. The big question: Who would succeed him—Harold, an English nobleman and the king's brother-in-law, or William, duke of Normandy and the king's cousin? Edward chose William, and sent Harold to Normandy to give William the news. On the journey, Harold was captured. To win his release, he promised he would be loyal to William and not contest the decision. To test his loyalty, William sent Harold to battle for him in Brittany. Harold was successful, and William knighted him. To further test his loyalty, William had Harold swear on the relics of the Bayeux cathedral that when Edward died, he would allow William to ascend the throne. Harold returned to England, Edward died...and Harold grabbed the throne.

William, known as William the Bastard, invaded England to claim the throne. Harold met him in southern England at the town of Hastings, where their forces fought a fierce 14-hour battle. Harold was killed, and his Saxon forces were routed. William—now "the Conqueror"—marched to London, claimed his throne, and became king of England (though he spoke no English).

The advent of a Norman king of England muddied the political waters and set in motion 400 years of conflict between England and France—not to be resolved until the end of the Hundred Years' War (1453). The Norman conquest of England brought that country into the European mainstream (but still no euros). The Normans established a strong central English government. Historians speculate that had William not succeeded, England would have remained on the fringe of Europe (like Scandinavia), and French culture (and language) would have prevailed in the New World—which would have meant no communication issues for us in France. Hmmm.

lands as ordered by William), and models of castles (who knew that the Tower of London was a Norman project?). Good explanations outline the events surrounding the invasion and the subsequent creation of the tapestry, and a touchscreen lets you see the back side of the embroidery.

Your visit finishes with a **film** that ties it all together one last time (in the cinema upstairs, skippable if you're pressed for time). Just before the theater you reach a full-sized replica of the tapestry (which you are welcome to photograph).

▲Bayeux Cathedral

This massive building, as big as Paris' Notre-Dame, dominates the small town of Bayeux. Make a point to enjoy the cathedral rising over the town after dark, when it's beautifully illuminated.

Cost and Hours: Free, daily July-Aug 8:30-19:00, Sept-June until 18:00, 4 Rue du Général de Dais.

Visiting the Cathedral: To start your visit, find the small **square** opposite the front entry (info board about the cathedral facade in rear corner). Notice the two dark towers—originally Romanesque, they were capped later with tall Gothic spires. The cathedral's west facade is structurally Romanesque, but with a decorative Gothic "curtain" added.

Now step inside the cathedral. The magnificent view of the **nave** from the top of the steps shows a mix of Romanesque (ground floor) and soaring Gothic (upper floors). Historians believe the Bayeux tapestry originally hung here. Imagine it draped halfway up the big Romanesque arches. Try to visualize this scene with the original, richly colored stained glass in all those upper windows. Rare 13th-century stained-glass bits are in the high central window above the altar; the other glass (below) is from the 19th and 20th centuries.

Walk down the nave and notice the areas between the big, round **arches.** That busy zigzag patterning characterizes Norman art in France as well as in England. These 11th-century Romanesque arches are decorated with a manic mix of repeated geometric shapes: half-circles, hash marks, full circles, and diagonal lines. Notice also the creepy faces eyeing you, especially the ring of devil heads lining the third arch on the right.

More 13th-century Norman Gothic is in the **choir** (the fancy area behind the central altar). Here, simple Romanesque carvings lie under Gothic arches whose characteristically tall, thin lines add a graceful verticality to the interior.

For maximum 1066 atmosphere, step into the spooky **crypt** (beneath the central altar), which originally was used as a safe spot for the cathedral's relics. The small crypt displays two freestanding columns and bulky capitals with fine Romanesque carvings. During a reinforcement of the nave, these two columns were replaced. Workers removed the Gothic veneer and discovered their true inner Romanesque beauty. Orange angel-musicians on other columns add color to this somber room.

Nearby: Leaving the church's front entry, walk around to the right and down a flight of steps. Look high on the church's spire to spy a little rectangular stone house. This was the **watchman's home,** from which he'd keep an eye out for incoming English troops during the Hundred Years' War...and for Germans five centuries later (it didn't work—the Germans took the town in 1940). Bayeux was liberated on D-Day plus one: June 7. According to an interesting (but likely false) legend, about the only casualty that day was the lookout, who supposedly was shot while watching from the window of this stone house.

The big tree ahead is a **Liberty Tree.** These were planted in cities throughout France in 1793 (when the king was beheaded) to celebrate the end of the Old Regime and the people's hard-won freedom. When the tree was planted, the cathedral kicked off a decade in which it was not considered a church but a revolutionary "temple of reason."

Place Charles de Gaulle

A block in front of the cathedral (up Rue Maîtrise) is a big, empty-yet-historic square—once the site of a 10th-century castle. The statue in the center is Poppa, the mistress or wife of the Viking conqueror Rollo who, in 911, became first duke of Normandy. The people of Normandy came from this union (not to mention many English royals—Rollo's descendants include William the Conqueror). On June 14, 1944, this square hosted the first public appearance of Charles de Gaulle in newly freed France. The self-appointed leader of the Free French Forces, now with Churchill's endorsement, proceeded to rally the French to rise up and help push out the Germans. This event helped initiate de Gaulle's legitimacy as head of the Free French. Bayeux later served as the first administrative capital of post-Nazi-occupied France.

River Walk

Join the locals and promenade along the meandering walking path that follows the little Aure River for about 2.5 miles through Bayeux. Find the waterwheel behind the TI to its right and keep walking (path marked on city maps).

Lace Conservatory (Conservatoire de Dentelles)

This conservatory offers a chance to watch workers design and weave intricate lace *(dentelle),* just as artisans did in the 1600s, when lace was an important Bayeux industry, competing to break the Venetian monopoly on this required bit of formal wear. Enter to the clicking sound of the small wooden bobbins used by the lacemakers, and appreciate the concentration their work requires. You can also see examples of lace from the past and pick up some nifty souvenirs. The community helps fund this teaching workshop to keep the tradition alive. The conservatory building is nicknamed the "Adam and Eve House" for its carved 15th-century facade (find Adam, Eve, and the snake).

Cost and Hours: Free, Mon-Sat 9:30-12:30 & 14:30-18:00 except Mon and Thu until 17:00, closed Sun, across from cathedral entrance, 6 Rue du Bienvenu, tel. 02 31 92 73 80, http://dentelledebayeux.free.fr.

▲MAHB (Musée d'Art et d'Histoire Baron Gérard)

For a break from D-Day and tapestries, MAHB offers a modest review of European art and history in a beautiful display space within what was once the Bayeux bishop's palace. The 14 rooms on two floors are laid out in chronological order (prehistory, ancient Rome, medieval, and early modern) and descriptions are translated into English. Bayeux was born during the Roman empire and you'll see ample evidence of that. In the stern Court of Justice—a courtroom from French revolutionary times (1793)—a bust of Lady Liberty (Marianne) presides over the tribunal like a secular goddess, backed by some Napoleonic stained glass (1806). You'll see a fine little collection of 18th- and 19th-century paintings donated by Baron Henri-Alexandre Gérard more than a century ago. Notable are an early work—*Le Philosophe (The Philosopher)*—by neoclassical master Jacques-Louis David and, by Antoine-Jean Gros, *Sappho*—a moonlit version of the Greek poetess' suicide that influenced Géricault and Delacroix. Lace lovers will enjoy several rooms of exquisite lace with drawers full of bobbins and artful creations. Your visit is capped with an exhibit dedicated to the ceramics of Bayeux.

Cost and Hours: €7.50, combo-ticket with other Bayeux museums, daily May-Sept 9:30-18:30, shorter hours off-season, near the cathedral at 37 Rue du Bienvenu, tel. 02 31 92 14 21, www.bayeuxmuseum.com.

Battle of Normandy Memorial Museum
(Musée Mémorial de la Bataille de Normandie)

This museum provides a manageable overview of WWII's Battle of Normandy. With its many maps and timelines of the epic battle to liberate northern France, it's aimed at military history buffs. You'll get a good briefing on the Atlantic Wall (the German fortifications stretching along the coast—useful before visiting Longues-sur-Mer), learn why Normandy was selected as the landing site, understand General Charles de Gaulle's contributions to the invasion, and realize the key role played by aviation. You'll also appreciate the challenges faced by doctors, war correspondents, and civil engineers (who had to clean up after the battles—the gargantuan bulldozer on display looks useful).

Cost and Hours: €7.50, combo-ticket with other Bayeux museums, daily May-Sept 9:30-18:30, Oct-Dec and mid-Feb-April 10:00-12:30 & 14:00-18:00, closed Jan-mid-Feb, last entry one hour before closing, on Bayeux's ring road, 20 minutes on foot from center on Boulevard Fabian Ware, free parking, tel. 02 31 51 25 50, www.bayeuxmuseum.com.

Film: A 25-minute film with original footage gives a good summary of the Normandy invasion from start to finish, and highlights the slog that continued even after the beaches were liberated (shown in English May-Sept at 10:30, 12:00, 14:00, 15:30, and 17:00; Oct-April at 10:30, 14:45, and 16:15).

Nearby: A right out of the museum leads along a footpath to

NORMANDY

the **Monument to Reporters,** a grassy walkway lined with white roses and stone monuments listing, by year, the names of reporters who have died in the line of duty from 1944 to today. Some years have been kinder to journalists than others. Notice how many names from recent years are Arabic.

The path continues to the **British Military Cemetery,** decorated with 4,144 simple gravestones marking the final resting places of these fallen soldiers. The cemetery memorial's Latin inscription reads, *"We Who Were Conquered by William Have Liberated His Fatherland."* Interestingly, this cemetery has soldiers' graves from all countries involved in the battle of Normandy (even Germany) except the United States, which requires its soldiers to be buried on US property—such as the American Cemetery at Omaha Beach.

Sleeping in Bayeux

Drivers should also see "Sleeping in Arromanches" (page 69).

NEAR THE TAPESTRY

$$$$ Villa Lara*** owns the town's most luxurious accommodations smack in the center of Bayeux. Most of the 28 American-size, spacious rooms have brilliant views of the cathedral (best after dark), and a few have small terraces. Hands-on owner Rima and her attentive staff take top-notch care of their guests (pricey but excellent breakfast, elevator, exercise room, comfortable lounges, free and secure parking, between the tapestry museum and TI at 6 Place de Québec, tel. 02 31 92 00 55, www.hotel-villalara.com, info@hotel-villalara.com).

$$$ Hôtel Churchill,* on a traffic-free street across from the TI, could not be more central, and owners Eric and Patricia are great hosts. The hotel has 46 plush-and-pricey rooms—some with traditional furnishings, and others quite modern. All have big beds and surround convivial public spaces peppered with historic photos of Bayeux's liberation (family rooms, 14 Rue St. Jean, tel. 02 31 21 31 80, www.hotel-churchill.fr, info@hotel-churchill.fr).

$$ Hôtel le Lion d'Or,* General Eisenhower's favorite hotel in Bayeux, draws a loyal American and British clientele who love the historic aspect of staying here. It has atmospheric Old World public spaces, 31 stylish rooms, and a responsive staff (no elevator, no air-con, limited but secure pay parking, restaurant with fair prices, 71 Rue St. Jean, tel. 02 31 92 06 90, www.liondor-bayeux.fr, info@liondor-bayeux.fr).

$$ Hôtel Reine Mathilde is a solid, centrally located value with 16 sharp rooms above an easygoing brasserie, and 10 pricier and larger rooms with three-star comfort in two annexes nearby (family rooms, some rooms with air-con, reception one block from

TI at 23 Rue Larcher, tel. 02 31 92 08 13, www.hotel-bayeux-reinemathilde.fr, info@hotel-bayeux-reinemathilde.fr).

¢ **Hôtel au Georges VII** offers 10 no-star, no-frills rooms (some with only a sink or a shower) with just enough comfort. The rooms are up a tight staircase above a central café, and the bartender doubles as the receptionist (19 Rue St. Martin, tel. 02 31 92 28 53, www.georges-7.com, augeorges7@orange.fr).

CHAMBRES D'HOTES NEAR THE CATHEDRAL

$$ Le Petit Matin, run by friendly Pascal, is a central and handsome bed-and-breakfast with good public spaces, five stylish rooms with big bathrooms, and a *magnifique* back garden (with play toys) on Place Charles de Gaulle (breakfast included, 9 Rue des Terres, tel. 02 31 10 09 27, www.chambres-hotes-bayeux-lepetitmatin.com, lepetitmatin@hotmail.fr).

$ Logis les Remparts, run by bubbly Christèle, is a delightful, three-room bed-and-breakfast situated above an atmospheric Calvados cider-tasting shop. The rooms are big and beautifully decorated in traditional style—one is a huge, two-room suite (breakfast extra, stays under €200 are cash only, a few blocks above the cathedral on parklike Place Charles de Gaulle at 4 Rue Bourbesneur, tel. 02 31 92 50 40, www.lecornu.fr, lecornu.bayeux@gmail.com).

$$ Manoir Sainte Victoire is a classy, 17th-century building with three top-quality rooms over a small garden at very fair prices (run by the friendly Bunels). Each has a small kitchenette and views of the cathedral (32 Rue de la Jurisdiction, tel. 02 31 22 74 69, mobile 06 37 36 90 95, www.manoirsaintevictoire.com, contact@manoirsaintevictoire.com).

NEAR PLACE ST. PATRICE

These hotels just off the big Place St. Patrice are a 10-minute walk up Rue St. Martin from the TI (a 15-minute walk to the tapestry).

$$ Hôtel d'Argouges*** (dar-goozh) is named for its builder, Lord d'Argouges. This tranquil retreat has a mini-château feel with classy public spaces, lovely private gardens, and 28 standard-comfort rooms. The hotel is run by formal Madame Ropartz and her son Frederick, who have renovated every aspect of the hotel (big family rooms, no elevator, secure free parking, just off Place St. Patrice at 21 Rue St. Patrice, tel. 02 31 92 88 86, www.hotel-dargouges.com, info@hotel-dargouges.com).

$ Hôtel Mogador** is a simple but good 14-room budget value with friendly owners. Choose between wood-beamed rooms on the busy square, or quiet but slightly faded rooms off the street. There are no public areas beyond the small breakfast room and tiny courtyard (20 Rue Alain Chartier at Place St. Patrice, tel. 02 31 92 24 58, www.hotelmo.fr, lemogador@gmail.com).

IN THE COUNTRYSIDE NEAR BAYEUX

$ La Ferme du Pressoir is a lovely, traditional B&B on a big work-ing farm immersed in the Norman landscape about 20 minutes south of Bayeux (see map on page 60). If you've ever wanted to stay on a real French farm yet rest in cozy comfort, this is the place. The five rooms are filled with wood furnishings and decorated with bright garden themes. Guests share a kitchenette, and larger groups can stay in a cottage with its own kitchen. The experience is vintage Normandy—and so are the kind owners, Jacques and Odile (good family rooms, includes good breakfast, Le Haut St-Louet, just off A-84, exit at Villers-Bocage, detailed directions on website, tel. 02 41 40 71 07, www.bandbnormandie.com, lafermedupressoir@bandbnormandie.com).

Eating in Bayeux

Drivers can also consider the short drive to Arromanches for sea-side dining options (see page 71). You're smart to book a day ahead for the **$$$** listings below.

ON OR NEAR RUE ST. JEAN

This traffic-free street is lined with cafés, *crêperies,* and inexpensive dining options.

$ Le Moulin de la Galette is like eating in an Impressionist painting. Enjoy a big selection of tasty crêpes, salads, and *plats* at good prices in a dreamy setting right on the small river. There's fine seating inside and out (effective heaters, closed Wed, 38 Rue de Nesmond, tel. 02 31 22 47 75).

$$$ La Rapière is a wood-beamed eatery—calm and roman-tic—filled with locals enjoying a refined meal and a rare-these-days cheese platter for a finale. Reservations are wise (closed Sun, 53 Rue St. Jean, tel. 02 31 21 05 45, www.larapiere.net, charming Linda).

$ Le Volet Qui Penche is a fun-loving, wine-shop-meets-bistro run by playful, English-speaking Pierre-Henri. He serves salads, escargot, *charcuterie*-and-cheese platters, and a small selec-tion of à la carte dishes as well as a vast selection of wines and cider by the glass (nonstop service until 20:00 most days—making early dinners easy, closed Sun, near the TI at 3 Passage de l'Islet, tel. 02 31 21 98 54).

$$$ L'Angle Saint Laurent is a tasteful and elegant place run by a husband-and-wife team (Caroline speaks English and man-ages the floor while Sébastien cooks). Come here for a special meal of *Normand* specialties done in a contemporary gourmet style. The selection is limited and changes with the season (good wine list, closed Mon, 2 Rue des Bouchers, reserve in advance, tel. 02 31 92 03 01, www.langlesaintlaurent.com).

$ Le Garde Manger, a family-friendly eatery, offers basic grub all day (omelets, big salads, pizza) with a marvelous outside terrace and cathedral views (daily 12:00-22:00, a block from Rue St. Jean at 23 Rue Larcher).

$$ Le Pommier, with street appeal inside and out, is a good place to sample regional products with clever twists in a relaxed yet refined atmosphere. Owner Thierry mixes old and new in his cuisine and decor, and focuses on organic food (good vegetarian *menu*, open daily, 38 Rue des Cuisiniers, tel. 02 31 21 52 10, www. restaurantlepommier.com).

$$$ Au P'tit Bistrot is a small, casual eatery with a snappy interior and a good reputation for its carefully prepared food. Warmly run by Magalie (whose husband is *le chef*), it's a mix of modern and traditional (closed Sun, 31 Rue Larcher, tel. 02 31 92 30 08).

$ La Fringale, nicely located on the main pedestrian street, is Bayeux's low-key diner with a big selection of basic café fare (closed Sun, 43 Rue St. Jean, tel. 02 31 22 72 52).

Bayeux Connections

From Bayeux by Train to: Paris' Gare St. Lazare (9/day, 2.5 hours, some change in Caen), **Amboise** (4/day, 5 hours, change in Caen and Tours' St-Pierre-des-Corps), **Rouen** (14/day, 2.5 hours, change in Caen), **Caen** (20/day, 20 minutes), **Honfleur** (2-3/day, 20-minute train to Caen, then 1-hour express PrestoBus—line #39—to Honfleur; more with train to Caen and scenic 2-hour ride on bus #20 via the coast; bus info tel. 02 31 89 28 41, www.busverts.fr), **Pontorson/Mont St-Michel** (3/day, 2 hours to Pontorson, then bus to Mont St-Michel; also consider Hôtel Churchill's faster shuttle van—described later).

By Bus to the D-Day Beaches: Bus Verts du Calvados offers minimal service to D-Day beaches with stops in Bayeux at Place St. Patrice and at the train station (schedules at TI, www.busverts. fr). Lines #74/#75 run east to Arromanches and Juno Beach (2-3/ day, afternoons only, none on Sun; 30 minutes to Arromanches, 50 minutes to Juno Beach), and line #70 runs west to the American Cemetery and Vierville-sur-Mer (2-3/day, afternoons only, none on Sun; 35 minutes to American Cemetery, 45 minutes to Vierville-sur-Mer). Going round-trip by bus often leaves you stuck with either too much or too little time at either sight; consider a taxi one way and a bus the other (for taxi information, see page 44).

By Shuttle Van to Mont St-Michel: Two services run shuttle-van day trips to Mont St-Michel for €65 round-trip (about 1.5 hours each way, plus at least 3 hours at Mont St-Michel): **Hôtel**

Churchill (hotel clients get a small discount; details at www. hotel-churchill.fr) and **Bayeux Shuttle** (www.bayeuxshuttle.com). Either trip is a terrific deal, as you'll get a free tour of Normandy along the way from your knowledgeable driver. Both run morning and afternoon trips when demand justifies.

D-Day Beaches

The 54 miles of Atlantic coast north of Bayeux—stretching from Utah Beach in the west to Sword Beach in the east—are littered with WWII museums, monuments, cemeteries, and battle remains left in tribute to the courage of the British, Canadian, and American armies that successfully carried out the largest military operation in history: D-Day. (It's called *Jour J* in French.) It was on these serene beaches, at the crack of dawn on June 6, 1944, that the Allies (roughly one-third Americans and two-thirds British and Canadians) finally gained a foothold in France. From this moment, Nazi Europe was destined to crumble.

> *"The first 24 hours of the invasion will be decisive... The fate of Germany depends on the outcome... For the Allies, as well as Germany, it will be the longest day."*
> —Field Marshal Erwin Rommel, April 22, 1944
> (from *The Longest Day,* by Cornelius Ryan)

June 6, 2014, marked the 70th anniversary of the landings. It was a huge deal here, given how few D-Day veterans are still alive. Locals talk of the last visits of veterans with heartfelt sorrow; they have adored seeing the old soldiers in their villages and fear losing the firsthand accounts of the battles. All along this rambling coast, locals will never forget what the troops and their families sacrificed all those years ago. A warm regard for Americans has survived political disputes, from de Gaulle to climate change agreements. This remains particularly friendly soil for Americans—a place where US soldiers are still honored and the image of the US as a force for good remains largely untarnished.

PLANNING YOUR TIME

I've listed the prime D-Day sites from east to west, starting with Arromanches (the British sector) and then the American sectors (with a stop-by-stop tour of Omaha Beach and its related sights, followed by Utah Beach). Finally, I backtrack east to cover the Canadian sector. In the British and Canadian sectors, overbuilding makes it harder to envision the events of June 1944, but the American sector looks today very much as it did 70 years ago. To best appreciate the beaches, avoid visiting at high tide if you can. For more information on touring the D-Day beaches, www.normandie-tourisme.fr is a useful resource.

NORMANDY

D-Day Sites in One Day

If you have only one day, I'd spend it visiting the exciting sites and impressive museums along the beaches and miss the Caen Memorial Museum. (To squeeze in the Caen Memorial Museum, visit it on your way to or from the beaches.) Note that the American Cemetery closes at 18:00 mid-April-mid-Sept and at 17:00 the rest of the year—and you'll want at least an hour there.

If you're traveling by car, begin on the cliffs above Arromanches. From there, visit the Port Winston artificial harbor and the D-Day Landing Museum, then continue west to Longues-sur-Mer and tour the German gun battery there. Spend your afternoon visiting the American Cemetery and its thought-provoking visitors center, walking on Omaha Beach at Vierville-sur-Mer, and exploring the Pointe du Hoc Ranger Monument. With an extra half-day, see the Utah Beach sights (to learn about the paratroopers' role in the invasion).

Canadians will want to start at the Juno Beach Centre and Canadian Cemetery (in Courseulles-sur-Mer, 10 minutes east of Arromanches).

Day-Tripping to the Beaches from Paris: If you're staying in Paris and considering a day trip to the D-Day beaches by train and rental car, think twice: Going by train to Caen, picking up a car, driving to your first stop, then returning to Paris will take at least seven hours. Note that Sunday train service to Bayeux is limited. A better alternative is to book a service to meet you at the Bayeux or Caen train station and drive you around the D-Day sites (see "By Taxi Minivan" and "By Minivan Tour," later). The Caen Memorial Museum also runs a good D-Day tour program for day-trippers.

GETTING AROUND THE D-DAY BEACHES
On Your Own

Though the minivan excursions listed below teach important history lessons, **renting a car** is a far less expensive way to visit the beaches, particularly for three or more people (for rental suggestions, see Bayeux's "Helpful Hints" on page 45).

Very limited **bus service** links Bayeux, the coastal town of Arromanches, and the most impressive sites of D-Day (see Bus Verts du Calvados info on page 57)—but it's not practical for anything more than one sight. **Bike riding** is dicey as roads are narrow (no bike lanes), with plenty of blind curves and relentless traffic.

NORMANDY

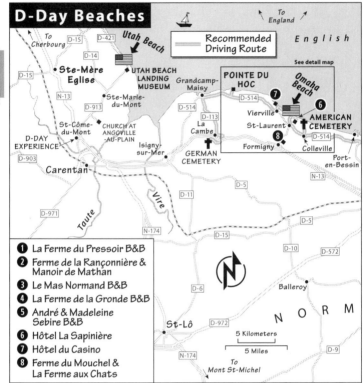

D-Day Beaches

Recommended Driving Route

❶ La Ferme du Pressoir B&B
❷ Ferme de la Rançonnière & Manoir de Mathan
❸ Le Mas Normand B&B
❹ La Ferme de la Gronde B&B
❺ André & Madeleine Sebire B&B
❻ Hôtel La Sapinière
❼ Hôtel du Casino
❽ Ferme du Mouchel & La Ferme aux Chats

By Taxi Minivan (Unguided)

Taxi minivans shuttle up to seven people between the key sites at reasonable rates (which vary depending on how far you go). Allow €240 for an eight-hour taxi day to visit the top Utah and Omaha Beach sites. No guiding is included; you are paying strictly for transport. Figure about €21 each way between Bayeux and Arromanches, €37 between Bayeux and the American Cemetery, and €100 for a 2.5-hour visit to Omaha Beach sites from Bayeux or Arromanches (50 percent surcharge after 19:00 and on Sun, taxi tel. 02 31 92 92 40 or mobile 06 70 40 07 96, www.taxisbayeux.com, taxisbayeux@orange.fr).

Abbeilles Taxis offer D-Day excursions from Caen (€200/5-hour visit, tel. 02 31 52 17 89, www.taxis-abbeilles-caen.com).

By Minivan Tour (Guided)

An army of small companies and private guides offers all-day guided excursions to the D-Day beaches. I've worked hard to find guides who respect the importance of your time and these sights. Anyone can get you around the beaches, but you should expect

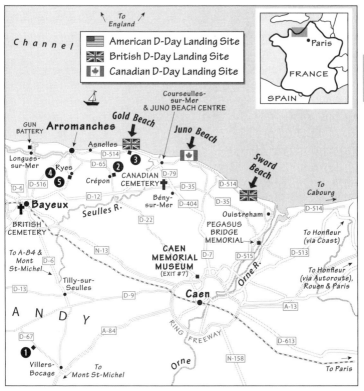

your guide to deliver clear history lessons and be at your side constantly. My recommendations meet and exceed these standards.

Most tours prefer to pick up in Bayeux; a few levy a small surcharge for a Caen pickup. Most guides skip Arromanches, prefer-

ring to focus on sights farther west: The "classic" itinerary run by most is Ste-Mère Eglise, Utah Beach, Pointe du Hoc, Omaha Beach, and the American Cemetery. The tour companies and guides listed here are people I trust to take your time seriously. Most deliver riveting commentary about these moving sites. (Most tours don't go inside museums.) To

land one of these guides, book your tour in advance (3-6 months is best during peak periods).

These tours are pricey because you're hiring a professional guide and driver/vehicle for the day. To spend less, look for a guide who will join you in your rental car. While you can save by hiring a guide for a half-day tour, a full day on the beaches is more satis-

Countdown to D-Day

1939

On September 1, Adolf Hitler invades the Free City of Danzig (today's Gdańsk, Poland), sparking World War II.

1940

Germany's Blitzkrieg ("lightning war") quickly overwhelms France, Nazis goose-step down Avenue des Champs-Elysées, and the country is divided into Occupied France (the north) and Vichy France (the south, administered by right-wing French). Just like that, nearly the entire Continent is fascist.

1941

The Allies (Britain, Soviet Union, and others) peck away at the fringes of "Fortress Europe." The Soviets repel Hitler's invasion at Moscow, while the Brits (with American aid) battle German U-boats for control of the seas. On December 7, Japan bombs the US naval base at Pearl Harbor, Hawaii. The US enters the war against Japan and its ally, Germany.

1942

Three crucial battles—at Stalingrad, El-Alamein, and Guadalcanal—weaken the German forces and their ally Japan. The victorious tank battle at El-Alamein in the deserts of North Africa soon gives the Allies a jumping-off point (Tunis) for the first assault on the Continent.

1943

More than 150,000 Americans and Brits, under the command of George Patton and Bernard "Monty" Montgomery, land in Sicily and begin working their way north through Italy. Meanwhile, Germany has to fend off tenacious Soviets on their eastern front.

1944

On June 6, 1944, the Allies launch "Operation Overlord," better known as D-Day. The Allies amass three million soldiers and six million tons of *matériel* in England in preparation for the biggest

fying. (These guides may do half-day trips: Bayeux Shuttle, Normandy Sightseeing Tours, Vanessa Letourneur, Edward Robinson, Rodolphe Passera, and Mathias Leclere—details for each next.)

Working with Your Guide: When hiring a private guide, take charge of your tour if you have specific interests (some guides can get lost in battle minutiae that you don't have time for). The best route for a one-day tour with a private guide is to start in Arromanches and end at Point du Hoc or the American Cemetery. Request extra time at the American Cemetery to see the excellent visitors center. While some companies discourage children, others (including Dale Booth, Normandy Sightseeing Tours, Mathias Leclere, Sylvain Kast, and Edward Robinson) welcome them.

fleet-led invasion in history—across the English Channel to France, then eastward toward Berlin. The Germans, hunkered down in northern France, know an invasion is imminent, but the Allies keep the details top secret. On the night of June 5, more than 180,000 soldiers board ships and planes in England, not knowing where they are headed until they're under way. Each one carries a note from General Dwight D. Eisenhower: "The tide has turned. The free men of the world are marching together to victory."

At 6:30 on June 6, 1944, Americans spill out of troop transports into the cold waters off a beach in Normandy, code-named Omaha. The weather is bad, seas are rough, and the prep bombing has failed. The soldiers, many seeing their first action, are dazed, confused, and weighed down by heavy packs. Nazi machine guns pin them against the sea. Slowly, they crawl up the beach on their stomachs. More than a thousand die. They hold on until the next wave of transports arrives.

Americans also see action at Utah Beach, while the British and Canadian troops storm Sword, Juno, and Gold. All day long, Allied confusion does battle with German indecision—the Nazis never really counterattack, thinking D-Day is just a ruse, not the main invasion. By day's end, the Allies have taken all five beaches along the Normandy coast and soon begin building two completely artificial harbors, code-named "Mulberry," providing ports for the reconquest of western Europe. The stage is set for the eventual end to the war.

1945

Having liberated Paris (August 26, 1944), the Allies' march on Berlin bogs down, hit by poor supply lines, bad weather, and the surprising German counterpunch at the Battle of the Bulge. Finally, in the spring, the Americans and Brits cross the Rhine, Soviet soldiers close in on Berlin, Hitler shoots himself, and—after nearly six long years of war—Europe is free.

Tours in a Shared Minivan

A few tour companies offer daily tours designed for individual sign-ups. Figure about €110/person for a day and €65/person for a half-day. (These companies also run private tours.)

Bayeux Shuttle is well-run and user-friendly for individuals. You can visit their office in Bayeux and usually book at the last minute. All departures are assured. Their vans have monitors explaining what's out the window, and they offer several all-day and half-day tours with well-trained guides (€60 half-day tour, €110 all-day tour including a good lunch, office open daily about 7:45-18:00, across from the Bayeux TI at Impasse de Islet, tel. 09 70 44 49 89, www.bayeuxshuttle.com).

NORMANDY

Normandy Sightseeing Tours delivers a French perspective with capable guides and will pick you up anywhere you like—for a price (€60 morning tour, €70 afternoon tour, €105 all-day tour, tel. 02 31 51 70 52, www.normandy-sightseeing-tours.com).

Overlord Tours is another good choice (www.overlordtour. com).

The Caen Memorial Museum runs a busy program of half- and full-day tours covering the American and Canadian sectors in combination with a visit to the museum (handy for those with limited time—see museum listing on page 90).

Tours with a Private Guide

Costs are about the same for all guides listed here. Private groups should expect to pay €500-650 for up to eight people for an all-day tour and €250-330 for a half-day.

Ex-Pat Guides: These (mostly British) guides, like a band of brothers, are passionate about teaching and offer excellent private tours. All have their own vehicles. While some are happy to ride in your car, let them do the driving. They work together and can help you find a guide if the first one you call is booked.

- **Dale Booth Normandy Tours,** led by Dale Booth (tel. 02 33 71 53 76, www.dboothnormandytours.com, dboothholidays@ sfr.fr).
- **D-Day Historian Tours,** with Paul Woodadge (mobile 07 88 02 76 57, www.ddayhistorian.com, paul@ddayhistorian. com).
- **First Normandy Battlefield Tours,** offered by Allan Bryson (www.firstnormandybattlefieldtours.com, firstnormandy@ sfr.fr).
- **Normandy Battle Tours,** led by Stuart Robertson (tel. 02 33 41 28 34, www.normandybattletours.com, stuart@ normandybattletours.com).
- **Battle of Normandy Tours,** guided by Edward Robinson (www.battleofnormandytours.com, edrobinson@ battleofnormandytours.com).

French Guides: These guides speak fluent English and are excellent teachers. Most have family connections to the area.

- **Rodolphe Passera** also guides at the D-Day Landing Museum at Utah Beach (mobile 06 30 55 63 39, www.normandy-americanheroes.com, normandyamericanheroes@gmail.com).
- **Sylvain Kast** (mobile 06 17 44 04 46, www.d-day-experience-tours.com, sylvainkast@yahoo.fr).
- **Vanessa Letourneur** can guide anywhere in Normandy (mobile 06 98 95 89 45, www.normandypanorama.com).
- **Mathias Leclere** (www.ddayguidedtours.com).

- **Magali Desquesne** (mobile 06 88 75 86 17, www.dday4you. com, mag.ddayguide@gmail.com).
- **Bertrand Soudrais** (www.executived-daytours.com).

HELPFUL HINTS

Good Booklet: A free visitor's guide gives succinct reviews of D-Day museums and sights with current opening times. It's available at TIs, but you usually need to ask for it (downloadable at www.normandie-tourisme.fr).

TV and Films About D-Day: D-Day guides recommend some preparatory viewing before your visit. The top two movies are *The Longest Day* (for the big D-Day story) and *Saving Private Ryan* (for a realistic sense of what it was like to land here and battle your way into France). *Band of Brothers,* a powerful 11-hour HBO miniseries telling the story from D-Day preparations, through the landing, and on to the end of the war, is simply the best.

Food Strategies: The D-Day landing sites are rural, and you won't find a grocery on every corner. Plan ahead if you want to picnic, or find groceries in Arromanches or Port-en-Bessin.

Tides: Tides will affect your experience of the beaches throughout the region, changing what you can see and your access to the sand. Avoid visiting the beaches at high tide if possible. Most TIs have tide tables to help you plan (when searching tide charts, the nearest reference point is Port-en-Bessin).

Arromanches

This small town—part of Gold Beach (in the British landing zone)—was ground zero for the D-Day invasion. The Allies decided it would be easier to build their own port than to try to take one from the Nazis. And so, almost overnight, Arromanches sprouted the immense harbor Port Winston, which gave the Allies a foothold in Normandy from which to begin their victorious push toward Berlin and the end of World War II.

A touristy-but-fun little town that offers a pleasant cocktail of war memories, cotton candy, and trinket shops, Arromanches makes a good home base for touring the D-Day beaches. Here you'll find an evocative beach, rusty hardware with English descriptions scattered around town, a good waterfront museum, a bluff with great views, and a theater with a thrilling little video. The town's pleasant seaside promenade is a great place from which to view the port.

Sit on the seawall after dark, listen to the surf, and contemplate the events that took place here almost 75 years ago.

Arromanches

English Channel

More of "Port Winston"
artificial harbor
in distance

Note: Map shows
beach at low tide.

Beach

RUSTED REMAINS
OF ARTIFICIAL
HARBOR

To
Longues-sur-Mer
via Coastal Path
(on foot only)

BEACHFRONT
PROMENADE

**D-DAY LANDING
MUSEUM**

HIGGINS BOAT &
PONTOON SECTION

Beach

RUE
JOFFRE

Pl. du 6 Juin 1944

SHERMAN
TANK

RUE DU COL. JOB

BLVD LONGUET

RUE COL
MICHEL

R. PETIT FONT

R. JOURDAN

RUE LAURENT

TOWER

PONTOON
SECTION

To
Courseulles-
sur-Mer,
Gold, Juno
& Sword
Beaches

CAMPGROUND

D-514

To Bayeux,
Longues-sur-Mer
& Omaha Beach

CHURCH

POST

**360
THEATER**

D-514

D-514

One-way
streets

D-22

200 Meters

200 Yards

To Caen

❶ Hotel Les Villas d'Arromanches
❷ Hôtel de la Marine
❸ Hôtel d'Arromanches &
   Restaurant "Le Pappagall"
❹ L'Hôtel Idéal de Mountbatten
❺ The Pub Mary Celeste
❻ Supermarket
❼ Arromanches Militaria Shop
   & Bakery

Orientation to Arromanches

Tourist Information: The service-oriented TI in the town center has a free leaflet illustrating the Port Winston harbor, bus schedules, a listing of area hotels and *chambres d'hôtes* (daily 10:00-12:00 & 14:00-17:00, July-Aug 9:30-12:30 & 13:30-18:30, 2 Avenue Maréchal Joffre, tel. 02 31 22 36 45, www.bayeux-bessin-tourisme. com). You may find a seasonal branch TI at the parking lot near the Arromanches 360° theater.

Arrival in Arromanches: The bus stop is at the top of the town across from the post office. The only pay parking in town is at the big parking lot by the D-Day Landing Museum (€.50/15 minutes, free 19:00-9:00). For free parking and less traffic, look for the lot between the small grocery store and L'Hôtel Ideal de Mountbatten as you enter town.

Services and Shopping: An **ATM** is at the post office, across from the museum parking lot. A small **market** is a long block above the beach, across from L'Hôtel Ideal de Mountbatten (closed Sun afternoon and Mon). **Arromanches Militaria** sells all sorts of D-Day relics and WWII paraphernalia (daily 10:00-19:00, in a

NORMANDY

tight space at 11 Boulevard Gilbert Longuet). To get an Arromanches-based **taxi,** call mobile 06 66 62 00 99.

Sights in Arromanches

Arromanches' key sight, the Port Winston artificial harbor, is best seen from two vantage points—above town on the bluff (with the Arromanches 360° theater), and from the seawall in town (near the D-Day Landing Museum).

▲▲▲Port Winston Artificial Harbor

Arromanches is all about its artificial harbor—the remains of which can be seen to this day. Winston Churchill's brainchild, the prefab harbor was made by the British and affectionately nicknamed Port Winston by the troops. To appreciate the massive undertaking of creating this harbor in a matter of days, start on the bluff overlooking the site of the impressive harbor. See the presentation at the cliff-top Arromanches 360° theater then head down to the D-Day Landing Museum and a nearby viewing area.

Getting to the Bluff: Drive two minutes toward Courseulles-sur-Mer and pay to park in the big, can't-miss-it lot overlooking the sea. Your other options are to hike 10 minutes from Arromanches' Center up the hill behind the town's D-Day Landing Museum, or take the free white tourist train from the museum (daily June-Sept, Sat-Sun only Oct-mid-Nov and April-May, none in winter, departures on the half-hour from below, on the quarter-hour from above). I'd train up and walk down.

Viewing the Harbor from the Bluff: Get close to the cliffs and survey the coast from this dramatic perch. To the left is the Ameri-

can sector, with Omaha Beach and then Utah Beach (notice the sheer cliffs typical of Normandy's coastline). Below and to the right lie the British and Canadian sectors (level landscape, no cliffs).

Along the beaches below, the Allies arrived in the largest amphibious attack ever, launching the liberation of Western Europe. On D-Day +1—June 7, 1944—17 old ships sailed 100 miles across the English Channel under their own steam to Arromanches. Their crews sank them so that each bow faced the next ship's stern, forming a sea barrier. Then 500 tugboats towed 115 football-field-size cement blocks (called "Phoenixes") across the channel. These were also sunk (with the ships and Phoenixes making a semicircle). This created a four-mile-long breakwater about a mile offshore. Finally, engineers set up seven floating steel pierheads with extendable legs, then linked these to shore with four floating roads made of concrete pontoons. (You'll see sections of pontoon roads at various locations along the beaches). Soldiers placed 115 antiaircraft guns on the Phoenixes and pontoons, protecting a port the size of Dover, England. Within just six days of operation, 54,000 vehicles, 326,000 troops, and 110,000 tons of goods had crossed the English Channel. An Allied toehold in Normandy was secure. Eleven months later, Hitler was dead and the war was over.

▲▲Arromanches 360° Theater

The domed building at the cliff-top houses the powerful film *Normandy's 100 Days*. The screens surrounding you show archival footage and photographs of the endeavor to liberate Normandy (works in any language). In addition to honoring the many Allied and German soldiers who died, it reminds us that 20,000 French civilians were killed in aerial bombardments. The experience is intense—as loud and slickly produced as anything at the D-Day beaches.

Cost and Hours: €6, €21.50 combo-ticket with Caen Memorial Museum; 2 shows/hour (on the hour and half-hour), daily May-Aug 9:30-18:00, April-May and Sept 10:00-18:00, Oct-mid-Nov 10:00-17:30, these are first and last show times, closed most of Jan, Chemin du Calvaire, tel. 02 31 06 06 45, www.arromanches360. com.

• *To return to the town center from the bluff, follow signs to* Musée du Débarquement—*the D-Day Landing Museum. The walk down is easy and delivers fine views and a Sherman tank (follow the small road in front of the Arromanches 360° theater).*

▲D-Day Landing Museum (Musée du Débarquement)

This museum, facing the harbor, makes a worthwhile hour-long visit and is the best way to appreciate how the artificial harbor was built. While gazing through windows at the site of this amazing undertaking, you can study helpful models, videos, and photographs illustrating the construction and use of the prefabricated harbor. Screens over the first big model show a virtual reconstruction of Port Winston. Those blimp-like objects tethered to the port prevented German planes from getting too close (though the German air force was largely irrelevant by this time). Ponder the overwhelming task of building this harbor in just 12 days, while battles raged. The essential 15-minute film (up the stairs behind the cashier) uses British newsreel footage to illustrate the construction of the port. Another video (7 minutes, far end of ground floor) recalls the night of the first landings.

Cost and Hours: €8, daily May-Aug 9:00-19:00, Sept until 18:00, Oct-Dec and Feb-April 10:00-12:30 & 13:30-17:00, closed

Jan, Place du 6 Juin, tel. 02 31 22 34 31, www.arromanches-museum.com.

Viewing the Harbor from near the Museum: Find the round bulkhead on the seawall, near the entrance to the D-Day Landing Museum. Stand facing the sea. Designed to be temporary (it was used for six months), the harbor was supposed to wash out to sea over time—which is exactly what happened with its twin harbor at Omaha Beach (which lasted only 12 days, thanks to a terrible storm). If the tide is out, you'll see rusted floats mired on the sand close in—these supported the pontoon roads. Imagine the traffic pouring in past the many antiaircraft guns poised to defend against the invasion.

On the hill beyond the museum, there's a partially viewable Sherman tank, one of 50,000 deployed during the landings. Stroll to the east side of the museum and find a section of a pontoon road, an antiaircraft gun, and a Higgins boat, which was used to ferry 30 soldiers at a time from naval ships to the beaches. Walk down to the beach and wander among the concrete and rusted litter of the battle—and be thankful that all you hear are birds and surf.

Sleeping in Arromanches

Arromanches, with its pinwheels and seagulls, has a salty beach-town ambience that makes it a fun overnight stop. For evening fun, do what most do and head for the small bar at Restaurant "Le Pappagall" (French slang for "parakeet") in the Hôtel d'Arromanches, or, for more of a nightclub scene, have a drink at the Mary Celeste Pub, around the corner on Rue Colonel René Michel.

Drivers should also consider my sleeping recommendations near Omaha Beach (see page 84).

$$$ Hotel Les Villas d'Arromanches*** has a privileged location, perched above the sea at the town's entry, a short walk to the center (easy and free parking). The original hotel has an attractive manor house feel with tastefully designed rooms, though plans are afoot to attach a new building in 2018 with more rooms, a spa, and a fitness room. Standard rooms are fairly priced, but you'll pay much more for rooms with views or a terrace (1 Rue du Lieutenant-Colonel de Job, tel. 02 31 21 38 97, www.lesvillasdarromanches.com, contact@lesvillasdarromanches.com).

$$ Hôtel de la Marine*** has a knockout location with point-blank views to the artificial harbor from most of its 33 comfortable rooms (family rooms, includes breakfast, elevator, view restaurant, Quai du Canada, tel. 02 31 22 34 19, www.hotel-de-la-marine.fr, hotel.de.la.marine@wanadoo.fr).

$ Hôtel d'Arromanches,** on the main pedestrian drag near the TI, is a good value, with nine small, straightforward rooms (some with water views), all up a tight stairway that feels like a tree house. Here you'll find the cheery, recommended Restaurant "Le Pappagall" run by English-speaking Luis (2 Rue Colonel René Michel, tel. 02 31 22 36 26, www.hoteldarromanches.fr, reservation@ hoteldarromanches.fr).

$ L'Hôtel Ideal de Mountbatten,*** located a long block up from the water, is a 12-room, two-story, motel-esque place with generously sized, stylish, clean, and good-value lodgings—and welcoming owners Sylvie and Laurent (family rooms, reception closed 14:00-16:00, easy parking—free if you book directly, short block below the main post office at 20 Boulevard Gilbert Longuet, tel. 02 31 22 59 70, www.hotelarromancheslideal.fr, contact@ hotelarromancheslideal.fr).

IN THE COUNTRYSIDE NEAR ARROMANCHES

$$ Ferme de la Rançonnière is a 35-room, country-classy oasis buried in farmland a 15-minute drive from Bayeux or Arromanches. It's flawlessly maintained, from its wood-beamed, stone-walled rooms to its traditional restaurant (good *menus* from €32) and fireplace-cozy lounge/bar (family rooms, bike rental, service-oriented staff, 4.5 miles southeast of Arromanches in Crépon, tel. 02 31 22 21 73, www.ranconniere.fr, ranconniere@wanadoo.fr).

The same family has two other properties nearby: The **$$ Manoir de Mathan** has 21 similarly traditional but bigger rooms a few blocks away in the same village (comparable prices to main building, Route de Bayeux, Crépon). An eight-minute drive away, in the village of Asnelles, are seven slick, glassy, modern seaside **$$ apartments** right along the beachfront promenade (2 Impasse de l'Horizon, www.gites-en-normandie.eu). For any of these, check in at the main hotel. Book directly so they can help you choose the property and room that works best for you.

$$ Le Mas Normand, 10 minutes east of Arromanches in Ver-sur-Mer, is the child of *Provençale* Mylène and *Normand* Christian. Here you get a warm welcome and the best of two French worlds: three lovingly decorated, Provence-style rooms wrapped in 18th-century Norman stone. The place is family-friendly with ample grass (family rooms, ask about their Gypsy-style trailer; includes breakfast; drive to the east end of little Ver-sur-Mer, turn right on Avenue de Provence, take another right where the road makes a T, and find the sign at 8 Impasse de la Rivière; tel. 02 31 21 97 75, www.lemasnormand.com, lemasnormand@wanadoo.fr).

$ La Ferme de la Gronde lies midpoint between Bayeux and Arromanches with five large traditional rooms in a big stone farmhouse overlooking wheat fields and lots of grass, with outdoor tables (includes breakfast, 2 big comfortable apartments ideal for families, well-signed from D-516 on Route de l'Eglise in Magnyen-Bessin, tel. 02 31 21 33 11, www.chambres-gite-normandie.fr, info@chambres-gite-normandie.fr).

At **¢ André and Madeleine Sebire**'s B&B, you'll experience a real Norman farm. The hardworking owners offer four modest, homey, and dirt-cheap rooms in the middle of nowhere (includes breakfast, 2 miles from Arromanches in the tiny Ryes at Ferme du Clos Neuf, tel. 02 31 22 32 34, emmanuelle.sebire@wanadoo.fr, little English spoken). Follow signs into Ryes, then go down Rue de la Forge (kitty-corner from the restaurant). Turn right just after the small bridge, onto Rue Tringale, and go a half-mile to a sign on the right to *Le Clos Neuf.* Park near the tractors.

Eating in Arromanches

You'll find cafés, *crêperies,* and shops selling sandwiches to go (ideal for beachfront picnics). The **bakery** next to the recommended Arromanches Militaria store makes good sandwiches, quiches, and tasty pastries. Many restaurants line Rue Maréchal Joffe, the bustling pedestrian zone a block inland. The following hotel restaurants are also reliable:

$$ Restaurant "Le Pappagall" serves basic café fare in a cheery setting (daily in high season, closed Wed and possibly other days off-season, see Hôtel d'Arromanches listing).

$$$ Hôtel de la Marine allows you to dine or drink in style on the water (great outdoor tables for a drink in nice weather, daily, see hotel listing).

Arromanches Connections

From Arromanches by Bus to: Bayeux (bus #74/#75, 2-3/day, none on Sun), **Juno Beach** (bus #74/#75, 20 minutes). The bus stop is near the main post office, four long blocks above the sea (the stop for Bayeux is on the sea side of the street; the stop for Juno Beach is on the post office side).

American D-Day Sites

The American sector, stretching west of Arromanches, is divided between Omaha and Utah beaches. Omaha Beach starts just a few miles west of Arromanches and has the most important sights for visitors. Utah Beach sights are farther away (on the road to Cherbourg), but were also critical to the ultimate success of the Normandy invasion. The American Airborne sector covers a broad area behind Utah Beach and centers on Ste-Mère Eglise.

Omaha Beach

Omaha Beach is the landing zone most familiar to Americans. This well-defended stretch was where US troops suffered their greatest losses. Going west from Arromanches, I've listed four powerful stops (and a few lesser ones): the massive German gun battery at Longues-sur-Mer (which secured the west end of the beach), the American Cemetery, Omaha Beach itself (at Vierville-sur-Mer, the best stop on the beach), and Pointe du Hoc.

• *The D-514 coastal road links to all the sights in this section—just keep heading west. I've provided specific driving directions where they'll help.*

▲Longues-sur-Mer Gun Battery

Four German casemates (three with guns intact)—built to guard

against seaborne attacks—hunker down at the end of a country road. The guns, 300 yards inland, were arranged in a semicircle to maximize the firing range east and west, and are the only original coastal artillery guns remaining in place in the D-Day region. (Much was scrapped after the war, long before people thought of tourism.) This battery, staffed by 194 German soldiers, was more defended than the better-known Pointe du Hoc. The Longues-sur-Mer Battery was a critical link in Hitler's Atlantic Wall defense, which consisted of more than 15,000 defensive structures stretching from Norway to the Pyrenees. These guns could hit targets up to 12 miles away with relatively sharp accuracy if linked to good target information. The Allies had to take them out.

Cost and Hours: Free and always open (and a good spot for a picnic); on-site TI open April-Oct daily 10:00-13:00 & 14:00-18:00. The TI's €5.70 booklet is helpful.

Getting There: You'll find the guns 10 minutes west of Arromanches off D-514 on Rue de la Mer (D-104). Follow *Port-en-Bessin* signs from Arromanches; once in Longues-sur-Mer, turn right at the town's only traffic light and follow *Batterie* signs to the free and easy parking lot (with WC).

Visiting the Battery: Walk in a clockwise circle, seeing the inland gun bunkers first and then the command bunker closer to the bluff before circling back to the parking lot. Enter the third bunker you pass. It took seven soldiers to manage each gun, which could be loaded and fired six times per minute (the shells weighed 40 pounds). Climbing above the bunker you can see the hooks that secured the camouflage netting that protected the bunker from Allied bombers.

Head down the path (toward the sea) between the second and third bunkers until you reach a lone observation bunker (look for the low-lying concrete roof just before the cliffs). This was designed to direct the firing; field telephones connected the observation bunker to the gun batteries by underground wires. Peer out to sea from inside the bunker to appreciate the strategic view over the Channel. From here you can walk along the glorious *Sentier du Littoral* (coastal path) above the cliffs and see bits of Arromanches' artificial harbor in the distance, then walk the road back to your car. (You can drive five minutes down to the water on the road that leads from the parking area.)

• *Continue west on D-514, passing two small sights of note—Port-en-Bessin and the Big Red One Museum—before arriving at the American Cemetery.*

Near Longues-sur-Mer
Port-en-Bessin

This sleepy-sweet fishing port west of Longues-sur-Mer has a historic harbor, lots of harborfront cafés, a small grocery store, and easy, free parking. Drive to the end of the village, cross the short bridge to the right, and park. While the old harbor was too small to be of use during the invasion, this was the terminus of PLUTO (Pipe Line Under the Ocean), an 80-mile-long underwater fuel

Hitler's Atlantic Wall

Germany defended its empire from Norway to the border of Spain with what Hitler called his "Festung Europa" (Fortress Europe), a supposedly impenetrable military shield, of which the so-called "Atlantic Wall" was a cornerstone.

German-controlled territory was growing from 1941 through 1942. But, after the Battle of Britain defeat, costly campaigns in Russia, the start of the Africa campaign, and the US entry into the war, things stalled for Germany. Rather than expanding, Hitler concentrated on consolidating. In 1942 he embarked on perhaps the greatest engineering project in history—fortifying (where necessary) almost 2,000 miles of European coastline in his Atlantic Wall.

Depending on the geography, Hitler strategically positioned huge gun batteries (to fire at ships up to 10 miles away) and smaller gun nests (about two per mile were needed—such as along the D-Day beaches). These bunkers had to evolve quickly as technology and Germany's situation changed. At first, the Germans had air superiority and could leave their guns in the open air. Then, in 1943, the Allies took control of the skies, and the German guns had to be built into heavily fortified bunkers.

A half-million people—mostly forced labor—worked furiously on the Atlantic Wall as D-Day approached, and German commanders wondered exactly where the Allies would strike.

line from England. This (and an American version that terminated at Ste-Honorine, one town over) kept the war machine going after the Normandy toehold was established.

Big Red One Museum

In humble Colleville-sur-Mer, this museum is a roadside warehouse filled with D-Day artifacts. This labor of love—one of many small D-Day museums in the area—is the life's work of Pierre, who for 30 years (since he was a boy) has been scavenging and gathering D-Day gear—and he is still finding good stuff. "Big Red One" refers to the nickname of the 1st Infantry Division, the US Army troops in the first wave (with the 29th Infantry Division) to assault Omaha Beach. Pierre is happy to show visitors around—his passion for his collection adds an extra dimension to your D-Day experience. Near the museum, the main street of little Colleville-sur-Mer is lined with WWII photos.

Cost and Hours: €5, June-Aug daily 9:00-19:00, spring and fall Wed-Mon 10:00-12:00 & 14:00-18:00, closed in winter, Le Bray, Colleville-sur-Mer, tel. 02 31 21 53 81.

▲▲▲WWII Normandy American Cemetery and Memorial

The American Cemetery is a pilgrimage site for Americans visiting Normandy. Crowning a bluff just above Omaha Beach, 9,386 bril-

liant white, marble tombstones honor and remember the Americans who gave their lives on the beaches below to free Europe. France has given the US permanent free use of this 172-acre site, which is immaculately maintained by the American Battle Monuments Commission.

A fine modern visitors center prepares you for your visit. Plan to spend at least 1.5 hours at this stirring site.

Cost and Hours: Free, daily 9:00-18:00, mid-Sept-mid-April until 17:00, tel. 02 31 51 62 00, www.abmc.gov. Guided 45-minute tours are offered a few times a day in high season (usually at 11:00 and 14:00—call ahead to confirm times). The best WC is in the basement of the visitors center.

Getting There: The cemetery is just outside Colleville-sur-Mer, a 30-minute drive northwest of Bayeux. Follow signs on D-514 toward Colleville-sur-Mer; at the big roundabout in town (at the Overlord Museum, described later), follow signs leading to the cemetery (plenty of free parking).

Visiting the Cemetery

From the parking lot, stroll in a counter-clockwise circle through the lovingly tended, parklike grounds, making four stops: at the visitors center, the bluff overlooking Omaha Beach, memorials to the fallen and the missing, and finally the cemetery itself.

Visitors Center: The low-slung, modern building is mostly underground. On the arrival level (after security check) are computer terminals providing access to a database containing the Roll of Honor—the names and story of each US serviceman whose remains lie in Europe.

The exhibit downstairs does more than recount the battle. It humanizes the men who fought and died, and are now buried, here. First find a large theater playing the video *Letters,* a touching 16-minute film with excerpts of letters home from the servicemen who now lie at rest here (shown on the half-hour, you can enter late). Next is a smaller, open theater with a moving eight-minute video, *On Their Shoulders.* From here, worthwhile exhibits and more videos (one includes an interview with Dwight Eisenhower) tell the stories of the brave individuals who gave their lives to liberate peo-

NORMANDY

ple they could not know, and shows the few possessions they left behind (about 25,000 Americans died in the battle for Normandy).

A lineup of informational plaques on the left wall provides a worthwhile and succinct overview of key events from September 1939 to June 5, 1944. Starting with June 6, 1944, the plaques present the progress of the landings in three-hour increments. Omaha Beach was secured within eight hours of the landings; within 24 hours it was safe to jump off your landing vehicle and slog onto the shore.

You'll exit the visitors center through the Sacrifice Gallery, with photos and bios of several individuals buried here, as well as those of some survivors. A voice reads the names of each of the cemetery's permanent residents on a continuous loop.

Bluff Overlooking Omaha Beach: Walk through a parkway along the bluff designed to feel like America (with Kentucky bluegrass) to a viewpoint overlooking the piece of Normandy beach called "that embattled shore, the portal of freedom." An orientation table looks over the beach and sea. Gazing at the quiet and peaceful beach, it's hard to imagine the horrific carnage of June 6, 1944. You can't access the beach directly from here (the path is closed for security)—but those with a car can drive there easily; see the Omaha Beach listing, later. A walk on the beach is a powerful experience.

• *With your back to the sea, climb the steps to reach the memorial (on the left).*

Memorial and Garden of the Missing: Overlooking the cemetery, you'll find a striking memorial with a soaring statue representing the spirit of American youth. Around the statue, giant reliefs of the Battle of Normandy and the Battle of Europe are etched on the walls. Behind is the semicircular Garden of the Missing, with the names of 1,557 soldiers who perished but whose remains were never found. A small bronze rosette next to a name indicates one whose body was eventually recovered.

Cemetery: Finally, wander through the peaceful and poignant sea of headstones that surrounds an interfaith chapel in the distance. Names, home states, and dates of death are inscribed on each tombstone, with dog-tag numbers etched into the lower backs. During the campaign, the dead were buried in temporary cemeteries throughout Normandy. After the war, the families of the soldiers could decide whether their loved ones should remain with their comrades or be

brought home for burial. (About two-thirds were returned to America.)

Among the notable people buried here are General Theodore Roosevelt Jr., his brother Quentin (who died in World War I but was moved here at the request of the family), and the Niland brothers (whose story inspired *Saving Private Ryan*). There are 33 pairs of brothers lying side by side, 1 father and son, 149 African Americans, 149 Jewish Americans, and 4 women. From the three generals buried here to the youngest casualty (a teen of just 17), each grave is of equal worth.

• *To visit Omaha Beach itself, return up the long driveway to the roundabout (at the Overlord Museum) and follow signs to St-Laurent-sur-Mer (D-514). But first consider popping into the Overlord Museum.*

Near the American Cemetery
Overlord Museum

While there are several museums more worth your sightseeing energy, you'll drive right by this purpose-built warehouse filled with Normandy's most impressive collection of WWII-era vehicles. Offering a good balance of American, British, and German exhibits, the museum's highlights include Germany's 88mm antiaircraft and antitank gun (formidable and feared by the Allies), a strafed German Panther tank (the best tank of the Third Reich), a Sherman tank, and a battlefield crane (recalling the on-the-go construction that took place in the field). You'll also see a horse—a reminder that much of the German war machine was actually powered by horses—and a Jeep, one of 640,000 made for the war.

Cost and Hours: €8, daily June-Aug 9:30-19:00, March-May and Sept 10:00-18:00, shorter hours off-season, closed Jan, tel. 02 31 22 00 55, www.overlordmuseum.com).

• *As you continue west on D-514 toward St-Laurent-sur-Mer, be on the lookout for...*

La Ferme de la Sapinière Calvados Tasting

La Ferme de la Sapinière is a stony apple farm welcoming guests with lots of free tastes along with a few photos of this family's (seven generations on this same farmstead) war experience. Drop-ins are welcome for tastings or you can join a one-hour tour in English that explains the growing, pressing, and fermenting of apples in Normandy (followed by tasting).

Cost and Hours: Open daily for tasting 9:30-19:30 except closed Sun Oct-March; tour/tasting-€3.50, April-mid-Nov Mon-Sat at 14:30, no tours on Sun, wise to call first; tel. 02 31 22 40 51, www.producteur-cidre.com. The farm is just off D-514 (Route de Port-en-Bessin) between the American Cemetery and St-Laurent-sur-Mer.

NORMANDY

On Omaha Beach

Walking on Omaha Beach is a powerful ▲▲▲ experience for history buffs. (While the beach is about 300 yards wide at low tide, it disappears at high tide.) Let the modern world melt away here and try to put yourself in those soldiers' combat boots:

You're wasted from lack of sleep and nervous anticipation. Now you get seasick, too, as you're about to land in a small, flat-bottomed boat, cheek-to-jowl with 29 other soldiers. Your water-soaked pack feels like a boulder, and your gun feels even heavier. The boat's front ramp drops open, and you run for your life through water and sand for 500 yards onto this open beach, dodging bullets from above (the landings had to occur at low tide so that mines and obstacles would be visible).

Omaha Beach witnessed by far the most intense battles of any along the D-Day beaches. The hills above were heavily fortified with machine gun and mortar nests. (The aerial, naval, and supporting rocket fire that the Allies poured onto the German defenses failed to put them out of commission.) A single German machine gun could fire 1,200 rounds a minute. That's right—1,200. It's amazing that anyone survived. It's estimated that on the first day of the campaign, the Allies suffered 10,500 casualties (killed, wounded, and missing), 6,000 of whom were Americans. The highest casualty rates occurred at Omaha Beach. More than 4,000 troops were killed and wounded here that day, many of whom drowned after being hit.

If the tide's out, you may notice remains of rusted metal objects just below the surface. Omaha Beach was littered with obstacles to disrupt the landings. Thousands of metal poles and "Czech hedgehogs," miles of barbed wire, and more than six million mines were scattered along this shore. At least 150,000 tons of metal were taken from the beaches after World War II, and they still didn't get it all. They never will.

• *From the farm, return to westbound D-514. At the next roundabout, follow signs to* Vierville s/Mer par la Côte *to get to Omaha Beach.*

Omaha Beach Sights from St-Laurent to Vierville

Omaha Beach has five ravines (or "draws"), which provided avenues from the beach past the bluff to the interior. These were the goal of the troops that day. You'll drive down one (Avenue de la Libération)—passing the small Omaha Beach Memorial Museum—to reach the beach and two commemorative statues. Then drive west along the beach to the National Guard Memorial before leaving the beach up a second ravine.

Omaha Beach Memorial Museum
(Musée Memorial d'Omaha Beach)

Skip the museum (for most visitors, it's not worth the entry), but WWII junkies should make a quick stop in the parking lot. On display is a rusted metal obstacle called a "Czech hedgehog"—thousands of these were placed on the beaches by the Germans to stop and immobilize landing craft and foil the Allies' advance. Find the American 155mm "Long Tom" gun nearby, and keep it in mind for your stop at Pointe du Hoc (this artillery piece is similar in size to the German guns that US Army Rangers targeted at that site). The Sherman tank here is one of the best examples of the type that landed on the D-Day beaches.

• You'll hit the beach at a roundabout. Park your car for a look at the two memorials, and to take a stroll on the beach. (If parking is tight or you want a quieter beach experience, turn right along the water and find a spot farther down along the road.)

▲▲Omaha Beach Focal Point

Omaha was the most difficult of the D-Day beaches to assault. Nicknamed "Bloody Omaha," nearly half of all D-Day casualties were suffered here.

Two American assault units landed on Omaha Beach—the 1st Infantry Division (the "Big Red One," a veteran formation) and the 29th Infantry Division (a National Guard citizen army unit with little combat experience). For those troops, everything went wrong.

The four-mile-long beach is surrounded on three sides by cliffs, which were heavily armed by Germans. The Allies' preinvasion bombing was ineffective, and about 500 Germans manning 11 gun nests pummeled the beach all day. Thanks to the concave shape of the beach, German artillery was positioned to hit every landing ship. It was an amphitheater of death.

Those who landed first and survived were pinned down, played dead, and came in with the tide over a period of four hours. Troops huddled against the beachhead for six to eight hours awaiting support—or death. But reinforcements kept coming. By the end of the day, 34,000 Americans had landed on the beach, and the Germans had been pushed back. In the next 34 days, these troops built 34 airfields. The final assault leading to Berlin was under way.

Memorial Statues

You're at the center of Omaha Beach. While only Americans landed on this beach, the flags recognize eight nations that took part in the invasion. A striking modern metal statue (*The Braves*, 2004) rises from the waves in honor of the liberating forces and symbolizes the rise of freedom on the wings of hope. Next to that is a much older memorial from 1949. Built by thankful French, it was funded by selling scrap metal after the war and honors the two assaulting divisions, the 29th and 1st. You can read the motto of the 1st Division: "No mission too difficult. No sacrifice too great. Duty first."

• *Drive west from here along the beachfront, nicknamed "Golden Beach" before the war for its lovely sand.*

Beachfront Drive

While movie images may give the impression that the D-Day beaches were wild, they were actually lined with humble beach hotels and vacation cottages much like those you see today. After about 250 yards, you'll pass a small memorial down on your left. This marks the site of the first temporary American cemetery (which was moved after about three days, as it provided a sad welcome to newly landed troops). If the tide is out, you'll see little skinny lakes between the sandbars. These were blood red on D-Day.

• *Drive until you reach a wharf stretching out from the Hôtel du Casino, at the base of the next ravine, where you'll find a couple of battlements and monuments. Park in one of two free lots and walk to the lower base of the boxy gray monument.*

National Guard Memorial

The 29th Infantry Division, a National Guard unit, was one of the American assault units that landed on Omaha Beach on D-Day. While well-trained and disciplined, these troops were less experienced than the battle-tested 1st Division, their landing partners. A memorial to their sacrifices is built atop an 88mm German artillery casement.

Look through the cage into the gun station. Rather than being aimed out to sea, this gun was aimed at the beach. It could shoot all the way across the beach in two seconds at the rate of two well-aimed shots per minute. Notice the desperate bullet holes all around the gun. Its twin was several miles away at the opposite end of Omaha Beach. In 1944 the Germans built this gun station and hid it inside the facade of a fake beach hotel. A second gun casement with two 50mm guns, a few steps to the west, added to the Omaha Beach carnage.

Walk up the steps to find another memorial. These two bronze soldiers commemorate the so-called "Bedford Boys" and the little Virginia town of Bedford that contributed 35 men to the landing forces—19 were killed.

Look out to the ocean. It was here that the Americans assembled their own floating bridge and artificial harbor (à la Arromanches; for a description, find the panel near the blue telescope).

The harbor was under furious construction for 12 days before being destroyed by an unusually vicious June storm (the artificial port at Arromanches and a makeshift port at Utah Beach survived and were used until November 1944).

NORMANDY

The nearby pier offers good views—handy if the tide is in. This is also a good place to walk along the beach.

• *From here, drive uphill on D-517 to return to coastal road D-514 at Vierville-Sur-Mer (as you head up, immediately look above and to your left to find two small concrete window frames high in the cliff that served as German machine gun nests).*

When you hit D-514, turn right (west) and head toward Pointe du Hoc. Along the way, just past the turnoff for the hamlet of Englesqueville la Percée (D-125), you'll have an opportunity to quench your thirst.

Lebrec Calvados Tasting

A 10th-century fortified farm on the left offers Calvados tastings. To try some, cross the drawbridge and park on the right. Ring the rope bell and meet charming owners Soizic and Bernard Lebrec. They're happy to offer a free three-part tasting: cider, Pommeau (a mix of apple juice and Calvados), and a six-year-old Calvados. Consider their enticing selection of drinkable souvenirs. Bernard likes to share his family's D-Day scrapbook (his farm was requisitioned as a military base in 1944). Ask to see the farm's own D-Day monument. Erected in September 1944—even before the war was over—it's likely one of the earliest in France (farm tel. 09 60 38 60 17).

• *Rejoin D-514, and at next roundabout, follow signs to Pointe du Hoc.*

▲▲▲Pointe du Hoc Ranger Monument

The intense bombing of the beaches by Allied forces is best understood at this bluff. This point of land was the Germans' most heavily fortified position along the Utah and Omaha beaches. The cliffs are so severe here that the Germans turned their defenses around to face what they assumed would be an attack from inland. Yet US Army Rangers famously scaled the impossibly steep cliffs to disable the gun battery. Pointe du Hoc's bomb-cratered, lunar-like landscape and remaining bunkers make it one of the most evocative of the D-Day sites.

Cost and Hours: Free, always open; visitors center open daily 9:00-18:00, mid-Sept-mid-April until 17:00, tel. 02 31 51 62 00, www.abmc.gov/cemeteries-memorials. It's off route D-514, 20 minutes west of the American Cemetery, in Cricqueville-en-Bessin.

Crowd Control: The sight is most crowded in the afternoons. Avoid 14:00-16:00 on peak days. And remember where you parked.

Visiting Pointe du Hoc

The only reason to enter the small visitors center is to see the eight-minute film explaining the daring Ranger mission from a personal perspective, through interviews with survivors. But if the security line is long, skip it, or save it for later.

Follow the gravel path to the site (with plenty of info panels focusing on individual Rangers). You'll pass through a short section of hedgerow before entering the cratered landscape. As you do, find the opening immediately on your left that's as wide as a manhole cover and about six feet deep. This was a machine gun nest with three soldiers crammed inside—a commander, a gunner, and a loader. From here, you'll circle the site counterclockwise with two battlements to climb around before winding your way back to the parking lot.

Lunar Landscape: The craters are the result of 10 kilotons of bombs—nearly the explosive power of the atomic bomb at Hiroshima—but dropped over seven weeks. This was a jumbo German gun battery, with more than a mile of tunnels connecting its battlements. Its six 155mm guns could fire as far as 13 miles—good enough to hit anything on either beach. For the American D-Day landings to succeed, this nest had to be

taken out. So the Allies pulverized it with bombs, starting in April 1944 and continuing until June 6—making this the most intensely bombarded of the D-Day targets. Even so, the heavily reinforced bunkers survived.

Walk around. The battle-scarred German bunkers and the cratered landscape remain much as the Rangers left them. You can crawl in and out of the bunkers at your own risk. There are three viewing platforms. Work your way to the bunker with the memorial at the edge of the bluff.

Dagger Memorial: The memorial represents the Ranger dagger used to help scale the cliffs. Here, it's thrust into the command center of the battery. Exploring the heavily fortified interior of this observation bunker (officers' quarters, enlisted quarters, and command room) with its charred ceiling and battered hardware, you can imagine the fury of the attack that finally took this station. The slit is only for observing. This bunker was the "eyes" of the guns—from here spotters directed the firing via hard-wired telephone, sending coordinates to the gunners at the six 155mm guns.

Walk down the steps to the front of the bunker for the greatest impact. Peer over the cliff and think about the 225 handpicked Rangers who attempted a castle-style assault on the gun battery. They used rocket-propelled grappling hooks connected to 150-foot ropes, and climbed ladders borrowed from London fire departments.

Timing was critical; the Rangers had just 30 minutes to get off the beach before the rising tide would overcome them. After reaching the clifftop, the Rangers found that the guns had been moved—the Germans had put telegraph poles in their place as decoys. The Rangers eventually found the operational guns hidden a half-mile inland and destroyed them.

Three American presidents (Eisenhower in 1963, Reagan in 1984, and Clinton in 1994) have stood at this bunker to honor the heroics of those Rangers.

Viewing Platform: Navigate the craters inland about 100 yards to another bunker capped with a viewing platform. Climb up top to appreciate the intensity of the blasts that made the craters and disabled phone lines—cutting communication between the command bunker and the guns to render them blind. Toward the western end of the site (where you can return to the parking area), you'll pass a big French 155mm gun barrel from World War I. While state-of-the-art in 1917, 27 years later—in World War II—this gun was still formidable. Six of these were what Pointe du Hoc was all about.

• *Our tour of the American Omaha Beach sights is finished. But to consider the other side of the conflict, it's worth visiting the **German Military Cemetery** at La Cambe. To get there from Pointe du Hoc, follow D-514 west, then turn off in Grandcamp following signs to La Cambe and Bayeux (D-199). After crossing over the autoroute, turn left at the first country road and follow it around to the cemetery.*

▲German Military Cemetery at La Cambe (Cimetière Militaire Allemand)

To ponder German losses, visit this somber, thought-provoking final resting place of 21,000 German soldiers. Compared to the American Cemetery at St-Laurent, this site is more about humility than hero appreciation. The largest of six German cemeteries in Normandy, it's appropriately bleak, with two graves per simple marker and dark basalt crosses in groups of five scattered about. The circular mound in the middle—with a cross, flanked by a grieving mother and father—covers the remains of about 300 mostly unknown soldiers.

Wandering among the tombstones, notice the ages of the soldiers who gave their lives for a cause some were too young to understand. "Strm" indicates storm trooper—the most ideologically motivated troops that bolstered the German army. About a fifth of the dead are unidentified, listed as "Ein Deutscher Soldat." You'll also notice many who died after the war ended—a reminder that over 5,000 German POWs perished in France clearing the minefields their comrades had planted.

A field hospital was sited in this area during the war, and originally American troops were buried here. After the war, those remains were moved to the current American Cemetery or returned to the US. A small visitors center, with a focus on building peace, displays the German soldiers' last letters home and a case of German artifacts. Visiting here, you can imagine the complexity of dealing with this for Germans.

Cost and Hours: Free, daily April-Oct 8:00-19:00, off-season generally 9:00-17:00, tel. 02 31 22 70 76.

Getting There: La Cambe is 15 minutes south of Pointe du Hoc and 20 minutes west of Bayeux (from the autoroute, follow signs reading *Cimetière Militaire Allemand*).

Sleeping near Omaha Beach

With a car, you can sleep in the countryside, find better deals on accommodations, and wake up a stone's throw from many landing sites. Besides these recommended spots, you'll pass scads of good-value *chambres d'hôtes* as you prowl the D-Day beaches. The last two places are a few minutes toward Bayeux on D-517 in the village of Formigny.

$$ Hôtel la Sapinière** is a find just a few steps from the beach at Vierville-sur-Mer. A grassy, beach-bungalow kind of place, it has 15 sharp rooms, all with private patios, and a light-hearted, good-value restaurant/bar (family rooms, outside St-Laurent-sur-Mer 10 minutes west of the American Cemetery—take D-517 down to the beach, turn right and keep going to 100 Rue de la 2ème Division D'Infanterie US, tel. 02 31 92 71 72, www.la-sapiniere.fr, sci-thierry@wanadoo.fr).

$$ Hôtel du Casino*** is a good place to experience Omaha Beach. This average-looking hotel has surprisingly comfortable rooms and sits alone overlooking the beach in Vierville-sur-Mer, between the American Cemetery and Pointe du Hoc. All rooms have views, but the best face the sea: Ask formal owner Madame Clémençon for a *côté mer* (elevator, view restaurant with *menus* from €30, café/bar on the beach below, Rue de la Percée, tel. 02 31 22 41 02, www.logishotels.com, hotel-du-casino@orange.fr). Don't confuse this with Hôtel du Casino in St-Valery-en-Caux.

At **$ Ferme du Mouchel,** animated Odile rents three colorful and good rooms with impeccable gardens in a lovely farm setting in the village of Formigny (cash only, includes breakfast, 3-day minimum in summer, tel. 02 31 22 53 79, mobile 06 15 37 50 20, www.ferme-du-mouchel.com, odile.lenourichel@orange.fr). Follow the sign from the main road (D-517), then turn left down the tree-lined lane when you see the *Le Mouchel* sign.

$ La Ferme aux Chats sits on D-517 across from the church in the center of Formigny and has welcoming owners, a cozy lounge with a library of D-Day information, and four clean, comfortable, modern rooms. Explore the sprawling gardens out back, with chickens, ducks, fish...and nine of those namesake cats (includes breakfast, tel. 02 31 51 00 88, www.lafermeauxchats.fr, info@fermeauxchats.fr).

Utah Beach

Utah Beach, added late in the planning for D-Day, proved critical. This was where two US paratrooper units (the 82nd and the 101st Airborne Divisions) dropped behind enemy lines the night before the invasion, as dramatized in *Band of Brothers* and *The Longest Day*. Many landed off-target. It was essential for the invading forces to succeed here, then push up the peninsula (which had been intentionally flooded by the Nazis) to the port city of Cherbourg.

Utah Beach itself was taken in 45 minutes at the cost of 194 American lives. More paratroopers died (over 1,000) preparing the way for the actual beach landing. Fortunately for the Americans who stormed this beach, it was defended not by Germans but mostly by conscripted Czechs, Poles, and Russians who had little motivation for this fight.

While the brutality on this beach paled in comparison with the carnage on Omaha Beach, many of the paratroopers missed their targets—causing confusion and worse—and the units that landed here faced a three-week battle before finally taking Cherbourg. Ultimately over 800,000 Americans (and 220,000 vehicles) landed on Utah Beach over a five-month period.

• *These sights are listed in the order you'll find them coming from Bayeux or Omaha Beach. For the first two, take the Utah Beach exit (D-913) from N-13 and turn right (see map on page 60).*

Church at Angoville-au-Plain

At this simple Romanesque church, two American medics—Kenneth Moore and Robert Wright—treated the wounded while battles raged only steps away. On June 6, American paratroopers landed around Angoville-au-Plain, a few miles inland of Utah Beach, and met fierce resistance from German forces. The two medics set up shop in the small church, and treated both American and German soldiers for 72 hours straight, saving many lives. German patrols entered the church on a few occasions. The medics insisted that the soldiers park their guns outside or leave the church—incredibly, they did. In an amazing coincidence, this 12th-century church is dedicated to two martyrs who were doctors.

A faded informational display outside the church recounts the events here; an English handout is available inside. Pass through the small cemetery and enter the church. Inside, several wooden pews toward the rear still have visible bloodstains. Find the new window that honors the American medics and another that honors the paratroopers.

Cost and Hours: €3 requested donation for brochure, daily 9:00-18:00, 2 minutes off D-913 toward Utah Beach.

▲▲▲Utah Beach Landing Museum (Musée du Débarquement)

This is the best museum located on the D-Day beaches, and worth the 45-minute drive from Bayeux. For the Allied landings to succeed, many coordinated tasks had to be accomplished: Paratroopers had to be dropped inland, the resistance had to disable bridges and cut communications, bombers had to soften German defenses by delivering their payloads on target and on time, the infantry had to land safely on the beaches, and supplies had to follow  the infantry closely. This thorough yet manageable museum pieces those many parts together in a series of fascinating exhibits and displays.

Cost and Hours: €8, daily June-Sept 9:30-19:00, Oct-Nov and Jan-May 10:00-18:00, closed Dec, last entry one hour before closing, tel. 02 33 71 53 35, off D-913 at Plage de la Madeleine, www.utah-beach.com. Park in the "obligitaire" lot, then walk five minutes to reach the museum.

Film and Tours: Check for the next English video time as you pay. Guided museum tours are offered twice a day: Call ahead for times or ask when you arrive (tours are free, tips appropriate).

Visiting the Museum

Built around the remains of a concrete German bunker, the museum nestles in the sand dunes on Utah Beach with floors above and below beach level. Your visit follows a one-way route past rooms of artifacts. It starts with background about the American landings on Utah Beach (over 20,000 troops landed on the first day alone) and the German defense strategy (Rommel was in charge of maintaining the western end of Hitler's Atlantic Wall—see the sidebar on page 74). See the outstanding 12-minute film, *Victory in the Sand*, which sets the stage.

Highlights of the museum are the displays of innovative invasion equipment with videos demonstrating how it all worked: the remote-controlled Goliath mine, the LVT-2 Water Buffalo and Duck amphibious vehicles, the wooden Higgins landing craft, and a fully restored B-26 bomber with its zebra stripes and 11 menacing machine guns, without which the landings would not have been possible (the yellow bomb icons painted onto the cockpit indicate the number of missions a plane had flown).

Upstairs is a large, glassed-in room overlooking the beach. From here, you'll peer over re-created German trenches and feel what it must have felt like to have been defending against such a massive and coordinated onslaught.

Outside the museum, find the beach access where Americans first broke through Hitler's Atlantic Wall. You can hike up to the small bluff, which is lined with monuments to the branches of military service that participated in the fight. A big gun sits atop a buried battlement, part of a vast underground network of German defenses. And all around is the hardware of battle frozen in time.

• *To reach the next several sights, follow the coastal route D-421 and signs to Ste-Mère Eglise.*

▲Ste-Mère Eglise

This celebrated village lies 15 minutes west of Utah Beach and was the first village to be liberated by the Americans. The area around Ste-Mère Eglise was the center of action for American paratroopers, whose objective was to land behind enemy lines before dawn on D-Day and wreak havoc in support of the Americans landing at Utah Beach that day.

For *The Longest Day* movie buffs, Ste-Mère Eglise is a necessary pilgrimage. It was in and near this village that many paratroopers, facing terrible weather and heavy antiaircraft fire, landed off-target—and many landed in the town. One American paratrooper dangled from the town's church steeple for two hours (a parachute has been reinstalled on the steeple where Private John Steele's became snagged). And though many paratroopers were killed in the first hours of the invasion, the Americans eventually overcame their poor start and managed to take the town. (Steele survived his ordeal and the war.) These troops who dropped (or glided) in behind enemy lines in the dark played a critical role in the success of the Utah Beach landings by securing roads and bridges.

Today, the village greets travelers with flag-draped streets (and plenty of parking). The 700-year-old **medieval church** on the town square now holds two contemporary stained-glass windows. One, in the back, celebrates the heroism of the Allies (made in 1984 for the 40th anniversary of the invasion). The window in the left transept features St. Michael, patron saint of paratroopers (made in 1969 for the 25th anniversary).

The **TI** on the square across from the church has loads of information (July-Aug Mon-Sat 9:00-18:30, Sun 10:00-16:00; Sept and April-June closes Mon-Sat 13:00-14:00 and Sun at 13:00; shorter hours off-season; 6 Rue Eisenhower, tel. 02 33 21 00 33, www.sainte-mere-eglise.info).

Museums in and near Ste-Mère Eglise
▲Airborne Museum
Housed in three buildings, this collection is dedicated to the daring aerial landings that were essential to the success of D-Day. During the invasion, in the Utah Beach sector alone, 23,000 men were dropped from planes or landed in gliders, along with countless vehicles and tons of supplies.

Cost and Hours: €8.50, daily May-Aug 9:00-19:00, April and Sept 9:30-18:30, shorter hours off-season and closed Jan, 14 Rue Eisenhower, tel. 02 33 41 41 35, www.airborne-museum.org.

Visiting the Museum: Your visit to the museum unfolds in three parts across three buildings. In the first building, you'll see a **Waco glider,** one of 104 such gliders flown into Normandy at first light on D-Day to land supplies in fields to support the paratroopers. Each glider could be used only once. Feel the canvas fuselage and check out the bare-bones interior. The second, larger building holds a **Douglas C-47** plane that dropped paratroops and supplies. Here you'll find mannequins of soldiers with their uniforms, displays of their personal possessions and weapons, and two movies: One focuses on the airborne invasion (20 minutes), and the other venerates President Ronald Reagan's 1984 trip to Normandy.

A third structure, labeled **Operation Neptune,** puts you into the paratrooper's experience starting with a night flight and jump, then tracks your progress on the ground past enemy fire using elaborate models and sound effects. Don't miss the touching video showing the valor of General Theodore Roosevelt Jr. on D-Day.

• *From Ste-Mère Eglise, head 10 minutes on N-13 (back toward Bayeux) to St-Côme-du-Mont.*

▲D-Day Experience
Just behind the Dead Man's Corner Museum is this new space dedicated to the paratroopers of the 101st Airborne Division. It's a labor of museum love, with lots of artifacts and uniforms capped by two creative experiences designed to help you feel what it might have been like to be in the 101st. First, enter the briefing room for a 10-minute review of your mission by a hologram commander. Then climb into an authentic Douglas C-47 (built in 1943, it actually flew on D-Day), buckle in, survive a simulated flight through

flak across the English Channel, then crash-land before you can parachute out.

Cost and Hours: €12, daily April-Sept 9:30-19:00, Oct-March 10:00-18:00, 2 Vierge de l'Amont (D-913), St-Côme-du-Mont, tel. 02 33 23 61 95, www.paratrooper-museum.org.

Canadian D-Day Sites

The Canadians' assignment for the Normandy invasions was to work with British forces to take the city of Caen. They hoped to make quick work of Caen, then move on. That didn't happen. The Germans poured most of their reserves, including tanks, into the city and fought ferociously for a month. The Allies didn't occupy Caen until August 1944.

Juno Beach Centre

Located on the beachfront in the Canadian sector, this facility is dedicated to teaching travelers about the vital role Canadian forces

played in the invasion, and about Canada in general. Canada declared war on Germany two years before the United States, a fact little recognized by most Americans today (after the US and Britain, Canada contributed the largest number of troops—14,000).

Cost and Hours: €7, €11 with guided tour of Juno Beach—highly recommended, daily April-Sept 9:30-19:00, Oct and March 10:00-18:00, Nov-Dec and Feb 10:00-17:00, closed Jan, tel. 02 31 37 32 17, www.junobeach.org.

Tours: The best way to appreciate this sector of the D-Day beaches is to take a tour with one of the Centre's capable Canadian guides, who will take you down into two bunkers and a tunnel of the German defense network (€5.50 for tour alone, €11 with admission, 45 minutes; April-Oct generally at 10:30 and 14:30, July-Aug also at 11:30, 13:30, and 16:30; verify times prior to your visit).

Getting There: It's in Courseulles-sur-Mer, about 15 minutes east of Arromanches off D-514. Approaching from Arromanches, as you enter the village of Grave-sur-Mer, watch for the easy-to-miss *Juno Beach–Mémorial* sign marking the turnoff on the left; you'll drive the length of a sandy spit (passing a marina) to the end of the road at Voie des Français Libres, where you'll find the parking lot.

Visiting Juno Beach Centre: The Centre includes many thoughtful exhibits that bring to life Canada's unique ties with Britain, the US, and France, and explains how the war front affected the home front in Canada. Your visit begins with a powerful, 12-minute film that captures Canada's D-Day experience. Next, you'll hear Canada's declaration of war against Germany on September 10, 1939, and learn about the various campaigns and heroism of Canadian soldiers and the immense challenges they faced during and after their landings here. A scrolling list honors the 45,000 Canadians who died in World War II and a large hall introduces visitors to the diversity of Canada. Take advantage of the Centre's eager-to-help, red-shirted "student-guides" (young Canadians working a seven-month stint here).

Nearby: Between the main road and the Juno Beach Centre, you'll spot a huge stainless-steel double cross (by a row of French flags). This is La Croix de Lorraine, marking the site where General de Gaulle returned to France (after four years of exile) on June 14, 1944.

Canadian Cemetery at Bény-sur-Mer

This small, touching cemetery hides a few miles above the Juno Beach Centre. To me, it captures the understated nature of Cana-

dians perfectly. Surrounded by pastoral farmland with distant views to the beaches, you'll find 2,000 graves marked with maple leaves and the soldiers' names and ages. Most fell in the first weeks of the D-Day assault. Like the American Cemetery, this is Canadian territory on French land.

Getting There: From Courseulles-sur-Mer, follow signs to Caen on D-79. After about 2.5 miles, follow signs to the cemetery (and Bayeux) at the roundabout. The cemetery is on Route de Reviers.

Caen Memorial Museum

Caen, the modern capital of lower Normandy, has the most thorough (and by far the priciest) WWII museum in France. Located at the site of an important German headquarters during World War II, its official name is Caen-Normandy Memorial: Center for History and Peace (Mémorial de Caen-Normandie: Cité de l'Histoire pour la Paix). With thorough coverage of the lead-up to World War II and of the war in both Europe and the Pacific, accounts of the Holocaust and Nazi-occupied France, the Cold War

aftermath, and more, it effectively puts the Battle of Normandy into a broader context and is worth ▲▲.

It's like a history course that prepares you for the D-Day sites, but it's a lot to take in with a single visit (which is why tickets are valid 24 hours). If you have the time and attention span, it's as good as it gets. If forced to choose, I prefer the focus of many of the smaller D-Day museums at the beaches (such as the Utah Beach Landing Museum).

Town of Caen: The old center of Caen is appealing and, with its château and abbeys, makes a tempting visit. But, I'd focus on Bayeux and the D-Day beaches. Bayeux or Arromanches—which are much smaller—make the best base for most D-Day sites, though train travelers with limited time might find urban Caen more practical.

The **TI** is on Place St. Pierre, 10 long blocks from the train station—take the tram to the St. Pierre stop (Mon-Sat 9:30-18:30, until 19:00 July-Aug, Sun 10:00-13:00 & 14:00-17:00 except closed Sun Oct-March, drivers follow *Parking Château* signs, tel. 02 31 27 14 14, www.tourisme.caen.fr).

A looming château, built by William the Conqueror in 1060, marks the city's center. To the west, modern Rue St. Pierre is a popular shopping area and pedestrian zone. The more historic Vagueux quarter to the east has many restaurants and cafés.

GETTING THERE

By Car: From Bayeux, it's a straight shot on the N-13 to Caen (30 minutes). From Paris or Honfleur, follow the A-13 autoroute to Caen. When approaching Caen, take the *Périphérique Nord* (ring-road expressway) to *sortie* (exit) #7—the museum is a half-mile from here. Look for white *Le Mémorial* signs. When leaving the museum, follow *Toutes Directions* signs back to the ring road.

By Train or Bus: By train, Caen is two hours from Paris (12/day) and 20 minutes from Bayeux (20/day). The modern train station sits next to the *gare routière*, where buses from Honfleur arrive (2/day express or 4/day via coastal route—see page 43). Car-rental offices are right across the street. There's no baggage storage at the station, though it is available (and free) at the museum.

Taxis usually wait in front of the train station and will get you to the museum in 15 minutes (about €17 one-way—more on Sun). A **tram-and-bus** combination takes about 30 minutes (Mon-Sat only): Take the tram right in front of the train station (line A, direction: Campus 2, or line B, direction: St. Clair; buy €1.30 ticket from machine and validate on tram and again on bus, good for entire trip). Get off at the third tram stop (Bernières), then transfer to frequent bus #2 (cross the street). For transit maps, see www. twisto.fr.

To return to the station, take bus #2 across from the museum (museum has schedule, buy ticket from driver and validate); transfer to the tram at the Quatrans stop in downtown Caen. Either line A or line B will take you to the station (Gare SNCF stop).

ORIENTATION TO CAEN MEMORIAL MUSEUM

Cost and Hours: €19.50, ticket valid 24 hours, free for all veterans and kids under 10 (ask about good family rates), €21.50 combo-ticket with Arromanches 360° theater (see page 68). Open March-Oct daily 9:00-19:00; Nov-Dec and Feb Tue-Sun 9:30-18:00, closed Mon; closed most of Jan (Esplanade Général Eisenhower).

Information: Tel. 02 31 06 06 44—as in June 6, 1944, www. memorial-caen.fr.

Planning Your Time: Allow a minimum of two hours for your visit. The museum is divided into two major wings: one devoted to the years before and during World War II, and the other to the Cold War years and later. Focus your time on the WWII wing.

Visitor Information: English descriptions are posted at every exhibit (but if you read every word, you'd be here for days). The €4 audioguide is well done and adds insight to the exhibits—a kid's version is also available.

Services: The museum provides free baggage storage and free supervised childcare for children under age 10. The large gift shop has plenty of books in English.

Eating: An all-day sandwich shop/café with reasonable prices sits above the entry area, and there's a restaurant with garden-side terrace (lunch only). Picnicking in the gardens is an option.

Minivan Tours: The museum offers good-value minivan tours covering the key sites along the D-Day beaches and is a top option for day-trippers from Paris. The all-day "D-Day Tour" package (€123) includes pickup/drop-off at the Caen train station, a tour of the museum followed by lunch, and a five-hour tour of the American sector (there's a similar tour option to Juno Beach). There's also a €90 half-day minivan tour that does not include the museum or lunch. Full-size bus tours run in summer (€49, June-Aug, no tours Tue or Sun, includes museum entry and half-day tour of the beaches). It is appropriate to tip these guides if you were satisfied with your tour.

VISITING THE MUSEUM

Find *Début de la Visite* signs and begin your museum tour here with a downward-spiral stroll, tracing (almost psychoanalyzing) the path Europe and America followed from the end of World War I to the rise of fascism to World War II. Rooms are decorated to immerse you in the pre-WWII experience.

The **"World Before 1945"** exhibits deliver a thorough description of how World War II was fought—from General Charles de Gaulle's London radio broadcasts to Hitler's early missiles to wartime fashion to the D-Day landings. Videos, maps, and countless displays relate the stories of the Battle of Britain, Vichy France, German death camps, the Battle of Stalingrad, the French Resistance, the war in the Pacific, and finally, liberation. Several powerful displays summarize the terrible human costs of World War II, from the destruction of Guernica in Spain to the death toll (21 million Russians died during the war; Germany lost 7 million; the US lost 300,000). A smaller, separate exhibit (on your way back up to the main hall) covers D-Day and the Battle of Normandy, though the battle is better covered at other D-Day museums described in this book.

Next, don't miss the 25-minute film, *Jour J (D-Day)—The Battle of Normandy,* an immersive, loud, and at times graphic black-and-white film covering the agonizing 100 days of the battle of Normandy (runs every half-hour 10:00-18:00, works in any language).

At this point, you've completed your WWII history course. Next comes the **"World After 1945"** wing, which sets the scene for the Cold War with photos of European cities destroyed during World War II and insights into the psychological battle waged by the Soviet Union and the US for the hearts and minds of their people until the fall of communism (you'll even see a real Soviet MiG 21 fighter jet). The wing culminates with an important display recounting the division of Berlin and its unification after the fall of the Wall.

Two more stops are outside the rear of the building. I'd skip the first, a re-creation of the former **command bunker** of German General Wilhelm Richter, with exhibits on the Nazi Atlantic Wall defense in Normandy. Instead, finish your tour with a walk through the **US Armed Forces Memorial Garden** (Vallée du Mémorial). On a visit here, I was bothered at first by the seemingly unaware laughing of lighthearted children, unable to appreciate the gravity of their surroundings. Then I read this inscription on the pavement: "From the heart of our land flows the blood of our youth, given to you in the name of freedom." And their laughter made me happy.

Mont St-Michel

For more than a thousand years, the distant silhouette of this island abbey has sent pilgrims' spirits soaring. Today, it does the same for tourists. Mont St-Michel, one of the top pilgrimage sites of Christendom through the ages, floats like a mirage on the horizon. For centuries devout Christians endeavored to make a great pilgrimage once in their  lifetimes. If they couldn't afford Rome, Jerusalem, or Santiago de Compostela, they came here, earning the same religious merits. Today, several million visitors—and a steady trickle of pilgrims— flood the single street of the tiny island each year. If this place seems built for tourism, in a sense it was. It's accommodated, fed, watered, and sold trinkets to generations of travelers who visit its towering abbey.

The easiest way to get to Mont St-Michel is by car, but various rail, bus, and minivan options are also available. France's national rail system SNCF recently started a faster TGV service to nearby Rennes, and Flixbus runs direct and cheap bus service to the island from Paris. Also, minivan shuttle services can zip you here from Bayeux. See "Mont St-Michel Connections" and "Bayeux Connections" for more.

Orientation to Mont St-Michel

Mont St-Michel is surrounded by a vast mudflat and connected to the mainland by a bridge. Think of the island as having three parts: the Benedictine abbey soaring above, the spindly road leading to the abbey, and the medieval fortifications below. The lone main street (Grand Rue), with the island's hotels, restaurants, and trinkets, is mobbed in-season from 11:00 to 16:00. Though several tacky history-in-wax museums tempt visitors with hustlers out front, these are commercial gimmicks with no real artifacts. The only worthwhile sights are the abbey at the summit and a ramble on the ramparts, which offers mudflat views and an escape from the tourist zone.

The "village" on the mainland side of the causeway (called La Caserne) was built to accommodate tour buses. It consists of a lineup of modern hotels, a handful of shops, vast parking lots, and efficient shuttle vehicles zipping to and from the island every few minutes.

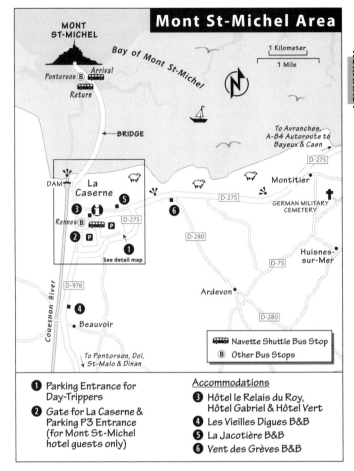

NORMANDY

Mont St-Michel Area

MONT ST-MICHEL

Bay of Mont St-Michel

Pontorson ⒷNavette Arrival

Navette Return

1 Kilometer

1 Mile

⟵ BRIDGE

To Avranches, A-84 Autoroute to Bayeux & Caen

D-275

DAM

La Caserne

⑤

③ ❶

Rennes Ⓑ Navette 🅿

❷ 🅿

❶

See detail map

Montitier

D-275

GERMAN MILITARY CEMETERY

❻

D-280

Huisnes-sur-Mer

D-75

D-976

Couesnon River

❹

• Beauvoir

Ardevon •

D-280

To Pontorson, Dol, ↓ St-Malo & Dinan

🚌 Navette Shuttle Bus Stop

Ⓑ Other Bus Stops

❶ Parking Entrance for Day-Trippers
❷ Gate for La Caserne & Parking P3 Entrance (for Mont St-Michel hotel guests only)

Accommodations
❸ Hôtel le Relais du Roy, Hôtel Gabriel & Hôtel Vert
❹ Les Vieilles Digues B&B
❺ La Jacotière B&B
❻ Vent des Grèves B&B

The tourist tide comes in each morning and recedes late each afternoon. To avoid crowds, arrive late in the afternoon, sleep on the island or nearby on the mainland, and depart early.

TOURIST INFORMATION

On the mainland, near the parking lot's shuttle stop, look for the excellent **visitors center** (daily April-Sept 9:00-19:00, off-season 10:00-18:00, www.accueilmontsaintmichel.fr). The official **TI** is on the island (just inside the town gate, daily July-Aug 9:15-19:00, March-June and Sept-Oct 9:15-12:30 & 14:00-18:00, shorter hours off-season; tel. 02 33 60 14 30, www.ot-montsaintmichel. com). A post office and ATM are 50 yards beyond the TI.

Either office is a good place to ask about English tour times for the abbey, bus schedules, and the tide table *(horaires des marées).*

An Island Again

In 1878, a causeway was built that allowed Mont St-Michel's pilgrims to come and go regardless of the tide. The causeway increased the flow of visitors, but blocked the flow of water around the island. The result: Much of the bay silted up, and Mont St-Michel was gradually becoming part of the mainland.

An ambitious project to keep it an island was completed in 2015. The first phase was the construction of a dam (barrage) on the Couesnon River, which traps water at high tide and releases it at low tide, flushing the bay and forcing sediment out to the sea. The dam is an attraction in its own right, with informative panels and great views of the abbey from its sleek and picnic-friendly wood benches. Parking lots at the foot of the island were then removed and a huge mainland parking lot built, with shuttle buses ferrying visitors to the island.

Finally, workers tore down the old causeway and replaced it with the super-sleek, artistically swooping bridge you see today. The bridge allows water to flow freely around Mont St-Michel, preserving its island character. Those wanting to experience Mont St-Michel at its natural best should plan their trip to coincide with high tide (see www.ot-montsaintmichel.com for tide tables).

ARRIVAL IN MONT ST-MICHEL

Prepare for lots of walking as the island—a small mountain capped by an abbey—is entirely traffic-free.

By Bus or Taxi from Pontorson Train Station: The nearest train station is five miles away in Pontorson (called Pontorson/Mont St-Michel). Few trains stop here, and Sunday service is almost nonexistent. Trains are met by buses that take passengers right to Mont St-Michel (€3, 12 buses/day July-Aug, 8/day Sept-June, fewer on Sun, 20 minutes, tel. 02 14 13 20 15, www.accueilmontsaintmichel.com). Or take a taxi to the shuttle stop (about €25, €30 after 19:00 and on weekends/holidays; tel. 02 33 60 33 23, mobile 06 32 10 54 06).

By Bus or Van from Regional Train Stations: Buses connecting with fast trains from Rennes and Dol-de-Bretagne stations drop you near the shuttle stop in the parking lot. From Bayeux, it's faster by shuttle van.

By Flixbus: Flixbuses leave from Paris' Gare de Bercy and stop in the huge parking lot near the shuttle stop (at the P7 parking area).

By Car: Day-trippers are directed to a sea of parking (remember your parking-area number). Expect parking jams in high season between 10:00 and noon. To avoid extra walking, take your

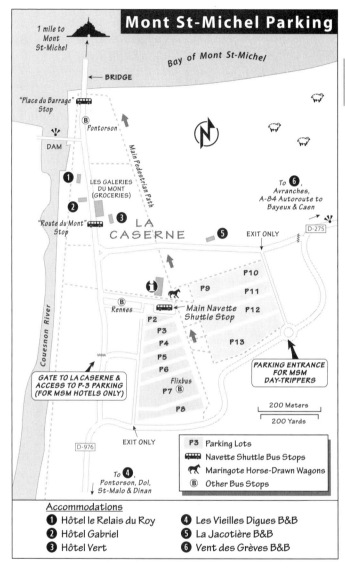

Mont St-Michel Parking

1 mile to Mont St-Michel

← BRIDGE

Bay of Mont St-Michel

"Place du Barrage" Stop

Pontorson

DAM

LES GALERIES DU MONT (GROCERIES)

"Route du Mont" Stop

LA CASERNE

EXIT ONLY

D-275

To **6**, Avranches, A-84 Autoroute to Bayeux & Caen

Main Pedestrian Path

Couesnon River

Rennes

P10

P9   P11

Main Navette Shuttle Stop   P12

P2

P3

P4   P13

P5

P6

Flixbus

P7

P8

GATE TO LA CASERNE & ACCESS TO P-3 PARKING (FOR MSM HOTELS ONLY)

PARKING ENTRANCE FOR MSM DAY-TRIPPERS

200 Meters

200 Yards

EXIT ONLY

D-976

To **4**, Pontorson, Dol, St-Malo & Dinan

P3 Parking Lots
Navette Shuttle Bus Stops
Maringote Horse-Drawn Wagons
B Other Bus Stops

Accommodations

1 Hôtel le Relais du Roy
2 Hôtel Gabriel
3 Hôtel Vert
4 Les Vieilles Digues B&B
5 La Jacotière B&B
6 Vent des Grèves B&B

parking ticket with you and pay at the machines near the visitors center (€11.70/up to 24 hours—no re-entry, €6.30/up to 2 hours, machines take cash and US credit cards, parking tel. 02 14 13 20 15). Parking is free if you arrive after 19:00 and stay only for the evening; if you arrive after 19:00 and leave before 11:30 the next morning, the fee is €4.

If you're staying at a hotel on the island or in La Caserne, you'll receive a parking-gate code from your hotel (ending with

"V"). As you approach the parking areas, follow wheelchair and bus icon signs until you come to a gate. Those staying on the island turn right here and follow signs for *Parking P3* (the parking is close to the shuttle bus, but you still pay €11.70 for 24 hours). Those staying at the foot of the island in La Caserne continue straight at the gate (enter your code), then drive right to their hotel (€4 fee per entry).

From the Parking Lot or La Caserne to the Island: You can either **walk** (about 50 level and scenic minutes) or pile onto the free and frequent **shuttle bus** (every few minutes, 12-minute trip). The shuttle makes four stops: at the parking lot visitors center, in La Caserne village, near the dam at the start of the bridge, and at the island end of the bridge, about 200 yards from the island itself. The return shuttle stop is about a hundred yards farther from the island (where the benches start). Most stops are unsigned—sleek wood benches identify the stops. Buses are often crammed. If it's warm, prepare for a hot (if mercifully short) ride. You can also ride either way in a horse-drawn *maringote* wagon (€5.50).

HELPFUL HINTS

Tides: The tides here rise above 50 feet—the largest and most dangerous in Europe. High tides *(grandes marées)* lap against the island TI door, where you should find tide tables posted (also posted at parking lot visitors center). If you plan to explore the mudflats, it's essential to be aware of the tides—and be prepared for muddy feet.

Baggage Check: The parking lot visitors center has lockers for bags, though they can be closed for security reasons—call ahead (see "Tourist Information," earlier).

ATM: You'll find one on the island just after the TI, at the post office.

Groceries: In La Caserne, **Les Galeries du Mont St-Michel** is stocked with souvenirs and enough groceries to make a credible picnic (daily 9:00-20:00).

Taxi: Call 02 33 60 33 23 or 02 33 60 26 89.

Guided Abbey Tours: Between the information in this book and the tours (and audio tours) available at the abbey, a private guide is not necessary.

Guided Mud Walks: The TI can refer you to companies that run inexpensive guided walks across the bay (with some English).

Crowd-Beating Tips: If you're staying overnight, arrive after 16:00 and leave by 11:00 to avoid the worst crowds. During the day you can skip the human traffic jam on the island's main street by following this book's suggested walking routes (under "Sights in Mont St-Michel"); the shortcut works best if you want to avoid both crowds and stairs. If you're here from mid-July through August, consider touring the abbey after dinner (it's open until midnight).

Best Light and Views: Mont St-Michel faces southwest, making morning light along the sleek bridge eye-popping. Early risers win with the best light and the fewest tourists.

After dark, the island is magically floodlit. Views from the ramparts are sublime. But for the best view, exit the island and walk out on the bridge a few hundred yards. This is the reason you came.

Sights in Mont St-Michel

The Bay of Mont St-Michel

Since the sixth century, the vast Bay of Mont St-Michel has attracted hermit-monks in search of solitude. The word "hermit" comes from an ancient Greek word meaning "person of the desert." The next best thing to a desert in this part of Europe was the sea. Imagine the desert this bay provided as the first monk climbed the rock to get close to God. Add to that the mythic tide, which sends the surf speeding eight miles in and out. Long before the original causeway was built, pilgrims would approach the island across the mudflat, aware that the tide swept in "at the speed of a galloping horse" (well, maybe a trotting horse—12 mph, or about 18 feet per second at top speed).

Quicksand was another peril. A short stroll onto the sticky sand helps you imagine how easy it would be to get stuck as the tide rolled in. The greater danger for adventurers today is the thoroughly disorienting fog and the fact that the sea can encircle unwary hikers. (Bring a mobile phone, and if you're stuck, dial 112.) Braving these devilish risks for centuries, pilgrims kept their eyes on the spire crowned by their protector, St. Michael, and eventually reached their spiritual goal.

▲▲Mudflat Stroll Around Mont St-Michel

To resurrect that Mont St-Michel dreamscape, it's possible to walk out on the mudflats that surround the island. At low tide, it's reasonably dry and an unforgettable experience. But it can be hazardous, so don't go alone, don't stray far, and be sure to double-check the tides—or consider a guided walk (details at the TI). You'll walk on mucky mud and sink in to above your ankles, so wear shorts and go barefoot. Remember the scene from the Bayeux tapestry where Harold rescues the Normans from the quicksand? It happened in this bay.

Village Walk Up to the Abbey

The island's main street (Grand Rue), lined with shops and hotels leading to the abbey, is grotesquely touristy. It is some consolation

NORMANDY

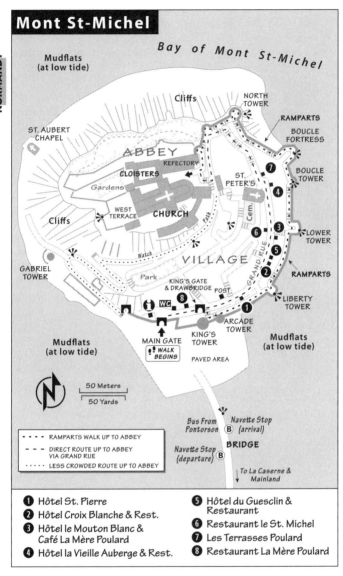

Mont St-Michel

Bay of Mont St-Michel

Mudflats
(at low tide)

Cliffs

NORTH
TOWER

RAMPARTS

BOUCLE
FORTRESS

ST. AUBERT
CHAPEL

ABBEY

REFECTORY

CLOISTERS

Gardens

WEST
TERRACE

Cliffs

CHURCH

ST.
PETER'S

BOUCLE
TOWER

7

4

6   **3**

LOWER
TOWER

5

VILLAGE

2

RAMPARTS

Watch

Park

GABRIEL
TOWER

GRAND RUE

KING'S GATE
& DRAWBRIDGE   POST

WC   **8**

LIBERTY
TOWER

1

ARCADE
TOWER

MAIN GATE

WALK
BEGINS

KING'S
TOWER

Mudflats
(at low tide)

PAVED AREA

Mudflats
(at low tide)

N

50 Meters

50 Yards

- - - - RAMPARTS WALK UP TO ABBEY

- - - DIRECT ROUTE UP TO ABBEY
VIA GRAND RUE

· · · · LESS CROWDED ROUTE UP TO ABBEY

Bus From
Pontorson   (B)

Navette Stop
(arrival)

Navette Stop
(departure)   (B)

BRIDGE

To La Caserne &
Mainland

1 Hôtel St. Pierre

2 Hôtel Croix Blanche & Rest.

3 Hôtel le Mouton Blanc &
Café La Mère Poulard

4 Hôtel la Vieille Auberge & Rest.

5 Hôtel du Guesclin &
Restaurant

6 Restaurant le St. Michel

7 Les Terrasses Poulard

8 Restaurant La Mère Poulard

to remember that, even in the Middle Ages, this was a commercial gauntlet, with stalls selling souvenir medallions, candles, and fast food. With only seven full-time residents (not counting a handful of monks and nuns at the abbey), the village lives solely for tourists.

To avoid the crowds, veer left as you approach the island's main entry and walk under the stone arch of the freestanding building. Follow the cobbled ramp up to the abbey. This is also the easiest route up, thanks to the long ramps, which help you avoid most stairs.

If you opt to trek up through the village on Grand Rue, don't miss the following stops:

Restaurant La Mère Poulard: Before the drawbridge, on your left, peek through the door of Restaurant La Mère Poulard. The original Madame Poulard (the maid of an abbey architect who married the village baker) made quick and tasty omelets here. These were popular with pilgrims who, back before there was a causeway or bridge, needed a quick meal before they set out to beat the tide. The omelets are still a hit with tourists—even at rip-off prices. Pop in for a minute just to enjoy the show as old-time-costumed cooks beat eggs. (When it comes to the temptation of an omelet on this island, I'd make like a good pilgrim and fast.)

King's Gate: During the Middle Ages, Mont St-Michel was both a fortress and a place of worship. The abbot was a feudal landlord with economic, political, and religious power. Mont St-Michel was the abbot's castle as well as a pilgrimage destination. Entering the town, you'll pass two fortified gates before reaching the actual village gate, the King's Gate, with its Hollywood-style drawbridge and portcullis. The old door has a tiny door within it, complete with a guard's barred window (open it). The other gates you passed were added for extra defensive credit. Imagine breaching the first gate and being surrounded by defensive troops. The highest tides bring saltwater inside the lowest gate.

Main Street Tourist Gauntlet: Stepping through the King's Gate, you enter the old town commercial center. Look back at the City Hall (flying the French flag, directly over the King's Gate). Climb a few steps and notice the fine half-timbered 15th-century house above on the right. (To skirt the main street crowds, stairs lead from here to the ramparts and on to the abbey—see "Ramparts" under the Abbey listing on page 107.) Once upon a time this entire lane was lined with fine half-timbered buildings with a commotion of signs hanging above the cobbles. After many fires, the wooden buildings were replaced by stone. As you climb, you'll see a few stone arches and half-timbered facades that pilgrims also passed by, five centuries ago.

St. Peter's Church (Eglise St-Pierre): At the top of the commercial stretch (on the left) is St. Peter's Church. A statue of Joan of Arc (from 1909, when she became a saint) greets you at the door. She's here because of her association with St. Michael, whose voice inspired her to rally the French against the English. St. Peter's feels alive (giving a sense of what today's barren abbey church might once have felt like). The church is dedicated to St. Peter, patron saint of fishermen, who would have been particularly beloved by the island's parishioners. Tour the small church counterclockwise. Just left of the entry is the town's only surviving 15th-century stained-glass window. In the far-left rear of the church (past its granite foundation) find the 1772 painting of pilgrims crossing the mudflat under the protection of St. Michael, who seems to be surfing on a devil's face over a big black cloud. To the right of the main altar lies the headless tomb of a 15th-century noblewoman (notice the empty pillow). During the Revolution heads were lopped off statues like this one, as France's 99 percent rose up against their 1 percent in 1789. From the center of the altar area, the fine carvings you see on the lectern and tall chairs are the work of prisoners held here during the Revolution. The church is busy with Masses (daily at 11:00 and special services for pilgrims).

Pilgrims' Stairs to the Abbey: A few steps farther up you'll pass a hostel for pilgrims on the right (Stella Maris, dark-red doors). Reaching the abbey, notice the fortified gate and ramparts necessary to guard the church entry back in the 14th century. Today the abbey, run by just a handful of monks and nuns, welcomes the public.

▲▲▲Abbey of Mont St-Michel

Mont St-Michel has been an important pilgrimage center since A.D. 708, when the bishop of Avranches heard the voice of Archangel Michael saying, "Build here and build high." Michael reassured the bishop, "If you build it...they will come." Today's abbey is built on the remains of a Romanesque church, which stands on the remains of a Carolingian church. St. Michael, whose gilded statue decorates the top of the spire, was the patron saint of many French kings, making this a favored site for French royalty through the ages. St. Michael was particularly popular in Counter-Reformation times, as the Church employed his warlike image in the fight against Protestant heresy.

This abbey has 1,200 years of history, though much of its story was lost when its archives were taken to St-Lô for safety during World War II—only to be destroyed during the D-Day fighting. As you climb the stairs, imagine the centuries of pilgrims and monks who have worn down the edges of these same stone steps. Don't expect well-furnished rooms; those monks lived simple lives with few comforts.

Cost and Hours: €10; May-Aug daily 9:00-19:00, until 24:00 Mon-Sat mid-July-Aug; Sept-April daily 9:30-18:00; closed Dec 25, Jan 1, and May 1; last entry one hour before closing; allow 20 minutes on foot uphill from the island TI, www.mont-saint-michel.monuments-nationaux.fr. Mass is held Mon-Sat at 12:00 and Sun at 11:15 (www.abbaye-montsaintmichel.com).

When to Go: To avoid crowds, arrive before 10:00 or after 16:00 (the place gets really busy by 11:00). In summer, consider a **nighttime visit:** You'll enjoy the same access for the same price with mood-lighting effects (bordering on cheesy) and no crowds (mid-July-Aug until 24:00, daytime tickets aren't valid for re-entry, but you can visit before 19:00 and stay on).

Tours: The excellent audioguide gives greater detail (€4.50, €6/2 people). You can also take a 1.25-hour English guided tour (free but tip requested, 2-4 tours/day, first and last tours usually around 11:00—10:45 on Sun—and 15:00, confirm times at TI, meet at top terrace in front of church). These tours can be good, but come with big crowds. You can start a tour, then decide if it works for you—but I'd skip it, instead following my directions, next.

❍ Self-Guided Tour: Your visit is a one-way route, so there's no way to get lost—just follow the crowds. You'll climb to the ticket office, then climb some more. Along that final stony staircase, monks and nuns (who live in separate quarters on the left) would draw water from a cistern from big faucets on the right. At the top (just past the WC) is a small view terrace, with a much better one just around the corner.

You've climbed the mount. Stop and look back to the church. Now go through the room marked *Accueil*, with interesting models of the abbey through the ages.

• *Emerging on the other side, find your way to the big terrace, walk to the round lookout at the far end, and face the church.*

West Terrace: In 1776, a fire destroyed the west end of the church, leaving this unplanned grand view terrace. The original extent of the church is outlined with short walls. In the paving stones, notice the stonecutter numbers, which are generally not exposed like this—a reminder that stonecutters were paid by the piece. The buildings of Mont St-Michel are made of granite stones quarried from the Isles of Chausey (visible on a clear day, 20 miles away). Tidal power was ingeniously harnessed to load, unload, and even transport the stones, as barges hitched a ride with each incoming tide.

As you survey the Bay of Mont St-Michel, notice the polder land—farmland reclaimed by Normans in the 19th century with the help of Dutch engineers. The lines of trees mark strips of land regained in the process. Today, the salt-loving plants covering this land are grazed by sheep whose salty meat is considered a local treat. You're standing 240 feet above sea level.

The bay stretches from Normandy (on the right as you look to the sea) to Brittany (on the left). The Couesnon River below marks the historic border between the two lands. Brittany and Normandy have long vied for Mont St-Michel. In fact, the river used to pass Mont St-Michel on the other side, making the abbey part of Brittany. Today, it's just barely—but definitively—on Norman soil. The new dam across this river was built in 2010. Central to the dam is a system of locking gates that retain water upriver during high tide and release it six hours later, in effect flushing the bay and returning sediment to a mudflat at low tide (see "An Island Again" sidebar on page 96).

• *Now enter the...*

Abbey Church: Sit on a pew near the altar, under the little statue of the Archangel Michael (with the spear to defeat dragons and evil, and the scales to evaluate your soul). Monks built the church on the tip of this rock to be as close to heaven as possible. The downside: There wasn't enough level ground to support a sizable abbey and church. The solution: Four immense crypts were built under the church to create a platform to support each of its wings. While most of the church is Romanesque (see the 11th-century

round arches behind you), the light-filled apse behind the altar was built later, when Gothic arches were the rage. In 1421, the crypt that supported the apse collapsed, taking that end of the church with it. None of the original windows survive (victims of fires, storms, lightning, and the Revolution).

In the chapel to the right of the altar stands a grim-looking 12th-century statue of St. Aubert, the man with the vision to build the abbey. Directly in front of the altar, look for the glass-covered manhole (you'll see it again later from another angle). Take a spin around the apse and find the suspended pirate-looking ship.

• *Follow Suite de la Visite signs to enter the...*

Cloisters: A standard abbey feature, this peaceful zone connected various rooms. Here monks could meditate, read the Bible, and tend their gardens (growing food and herbs for medicine). The great view window is enjoyable today (what's the tide doing?), but was not part of the original design. The more secluded a monk could be, the closer he was to God. (A cloister, by definition, is an enclosed place.) Notice how the columns are staggered. This efficient design allowed the cloisters to be supported with less building material (a top priority, given the difficulty of transporting stone this high up). Carvings above the columns feature various plants and heighten the cloister's Garden-of-Eden ambience. The statues of various saints, carved among some columns, were defaced—literally—by French revolutionaries.

• *Continue on to the...*

Refectory: At its peak, the abbey was home to about 50 monks. This was the dining hall where they consumed both food and the word of God in near silence as one monk read in a monotone from the Bible during meals (pulpit on the right near the far end). The monks gathered as a family here in one undivided space under one big arch (an impressive engineering feat in its day). The abbot ate at the head table; guests sat at the table below the cross. The clever columns are thin but very deep, allowing maximum light and solid support. From 966 until 2001, this was a Benedictine abbey. In 2001, the last three Benedictine monks checked out, and a new order of monks from Paris took over.

• *Stairs lead down one flight to a...*

Stone Relief of St. Michael: This romanticized scene (carved in 1860) depicts the legend of Mont St-Michel: The archangel Michael wanted to commemorate a hard-fought victory over the devil with the construction of a monumental abbey on a nearby island. He sent his message to the bishop of Avranches—St. Aubert—who saw Michael twice in his dreams. But the bishop didn't trust his dreams until the third time, when Michael drove his thumb into the bishop's head, leaving a mark that he could not ignore. Notice the urgent gesture of Michael's hand and arm as the saint points to the uninhabited mount. The bishop finally got the message, and the first chapel was consecrated in 709.

• *Continue down the stairs another flight to the...*

Guests' Hall: St. Benedict wrote that guests should be welcomed according to their status. That meant that when kings (or other VIPs) visited, they were wined and dined without a hint of monastic austerity. This room once exploded in color, with gold stars on a blue sky across the ceiling. (This room's decoration was said to be the model for Sainte-Chapelle in Paris.) The floor was composed of glazed red-and-green tiles. The entire space was bathed in glorious sunlight, made divine as it passed through a filter of stained glass. The big double fireplace, kept out of sight by hanging tapestries, served as a kitchen—walk under it, imagine an entire wild boar on a spit, and see the light.

• *Hike up the stairs through a chapel to the...*

Hall of the Grand Pillars: Perched on a pointy rock, the huge abbey church had four sturdy crypts like this to prop it up. You're standing under the Gothic portion of the abbey church—this was the crypt that collapsed in 1421. Notice the immensity of the columns (15 feet around) in the new crypt, rebuilt with a determination not to let it fall again. Now look up at the round hole in the ceiling and recognize it as the glass "manhole cover" from the church altar above.

• *To see what kind of crypt collapsed, continue on to the...*

Crypt of St. Martin: This simple 11th-century vault, one of the oldest on the mount, is textbook Romanesque. It has minimal openings, since the walls needed to be solid and fat to support the buildings above. As you leave, notice the thickness of the walls.

• *Walking on, study the barnacle-like unplanned stone construction, added haphazardly over the centuries, yet all integrated. Next, you'll find the...*

Ossuary (identifiable by its big treadwheel): The monks celebrated death as well as life. This part of the abbey housed the hospital, morgue, and ossuary. Because the abbey graveyard was small, it was routinely emptied, and the bones were stacked here.

During the Revolution, monasticism was abolished. Church property was taken by the secular government, and from 1793 to 1863, Mont St-Michel was used as an Alcatraz-type prison. Its first inmates were 300 priests who refused to renounce their vows. (Victor Hugo complained that using such a place as a prison was like keeping a toad in a reliquary.) The big treadwheel from 1820—the kind that did heavy lifting for big building projects throughout the Middle Ages—is from the decades when the abbey was a prison. Teams of six prisoners marched two abreast in the wheel, hamster-style, powering two-ton loads of stone and supplies up Mont St-Michel. Spin the rollers of the sled next to the wheel.

From here, you'll pass through a chapel (with a rare fragment of a 13th-century fresco above), walk up the Romanesque-arched North-South Stairs, pass through the Promenade of the Monks (appreciate the fine medieval stonework, built directly into the granite rock of the island), go under more Gothic vaults, and finally descend into the vast...

Scriptorium Hall (a.k.a. Knights Hall): This important room is where monks decorated illuminated manuscripts and transcribed texts. It faces north so its big windows would let in lots of flat, indirect light, the preference of artists throughout time. You'll then spiral down to the gift shop, exiting out the back door (follow signs to the *Jardins*).

• *You'll emerge into the rear garden. From here, look back from where you just came and up at a miracle (merveille) of medieval engineering.*

The "Merveille": This was an immense building project—a marvel back in 1220. Three levels of buildings were created: the lower floor for storage, the middle floor for work and study, and the top floor for meditation (in the cloister, open to the heavens). It was a medieval skyscraper. The vision was even grander—the place where you're standing was to be built up in similar fashion to support an expansion of the church. But the money ran out, and the project was abandoned. As you leave the garden, notice the tall narrow windows of the refectory on the top floor.

• *Exiting the abbey, you'll pop out midway on the steps you climbed to get here. You could descend here straight into tourist Hell. But for a little rampart romance, go down only until you find the short stairway on the left. Climb up the dozen steps and circle right, following a well-fortified outer rampart with a few awe-inspiring viewpoints before heading back down to the King's Gate and the bridge. (From near the high point, try to spot the former schoolhouse—operational until 1972—with its school bell, small playground, and tree.)*

NORMANDY

Ramparts: Mont St-Michel is ringed by a fine example of 15th-century fortifications. They were built to defend against a new weapon: the cannon. They were low, rather than tall—to make a smaller target—and connected by protected passageways, which enabled soldiers to zip quickly to whichever zone was under attack. The five-sided Boucle Tower (1481) was crafted with no blind angles, so defenders could protect it and the nearby walls in all directions. And though the English conquered all of Normandy in the early 15th century, they never took this well-fortified island. Because of its stubborn success against the English in the Hundred Years' War, Mont St-Michel became a symbol of French national identity.

NEAR MONT ST-MICHEL
German Military Cemetery (Cimetière Militaire Allemand)
Located three miles from Mont St-Michel, near tiny Huisnes-sur-Mer, this somber cemetery-mortuary houses the remains of 12,000 German WWII soldiers brought to this location from all over France. The stone blocks on the steps up indicate the regions in France from where they came. From the upstairs lookout, take in the sensational views over Mont St-Michel. The cemetery is well-signed east of Mont St-Michel (off D-275 at 3 Rue du Mont de Huisnes).

Sleeping in Mont St-Michel

Sleep on or near the island so that you can visit Mont St-Michel early and late. What matters is being here before or after the crush of tourists, and seeing the island floodlit after dark. Sleeping on the island—inside the walls—is a memorable experience for medieval romantics who don't mind small and overpriced rooms of average quality, and baggage hassles. To reach a room on the island, you'll need to carry your bags 15 minutes from the *navette* (shuttle) stop. Take only what you need for one night in a smaller bag, but don't leave any luggage visible in your car.

Hotels and *chambres d'hôtes* near the island are a better value (if less romantic). Those listed below are within walking distance of the free and frequent shuttle to the island.

ON THE ISLAND

Because most visitors day-trip here, finding a room is generally no problem. Though some pad their profits by requesting that guests buy dinner from their restaurant, requiring it is illegal. Higher-priced rooms generally have bay views.

The following hotels, all on Grand Rue, are listed in order of altitude from lowest to highest.

$$$$ Hôtel St. Pierre* and **Hôtel Croix Blanche*** sit side by side and share the same owners and reception desk (at St. Pierre). Each provides comfortable rooms at inflated prices, some with good views (family rooms, lower rates at Hôtel Croix Blanche, tel. 02 33 60 14 03, www.auberge-saint-pierre.fr, contact@auberge-saint-pierre.fr).

$$$ Hôtel le Mouton Blanc* delivers a fair midrange value, with 15 rooms split between two buildings. Rooms in the main building have wood beams. The entire hotel is being renovated for the 2018 season, so rooms should be fresh when you visit (tel. 02 33 60 14 08, www.lemoutonblanc.fr, contact@lemoutonblanc.fr).

$$ Hôtel la Vieille Auberge* is a small place with good rooms at fair prices (pricier but worthwhile view room with deck; check in at their restaurant, but book through Hôtel St. Pierre, listed above).

$$ Hôtel du Guesclin* has the cheapest and best-value rooms I list on the island and is the only family-run hotel left there. Rooms have simple decor and provide basic comfort (tel. 02 33 60 14 10, www.hotelduguesclin.com, hotel.duguesclin@wanadoo.fr).

ON THE MAINLAND

Modern hotels with easy parking and quick shuttle-bus access gather in La Caserne near the bridge to the island.

$$ Hôtel le Relais du Roy* houses small but well-configured and plush rooms above nice public spaces. Most rooms are on the riverside, with countryside views, and many have small balconies allowing "lean-out" views to the abbey (bar, restaurant, 8 Route du Mont Saint-Michel, tel. 02 33 60 14 25, www.le-relais-du-roy.com, reservation@le-relais-du-roy.com).

$$ Hôtel Gabriel* has 45 modern rooms, both bright and tight, with flashy colors and fair rates (includes breakfast, Route du Mont Saint-Michel, tel. 02 33 60 14 13, www.hotelgabriel-montsaintmichel.com, hotelgabriel@le-mont-saint-michel.com).

$ Hôtel Vert* provides 54 motel-esque rooms at good rates (family rooms, Route du Mont Saint-Michel, tel. 02 33 60 09 33, www.hotelvert-montsaintmichel.com, stmichel@le-mont-saint-michel.com).

CHAMBRES D'HOTES

Simply great values, these places are a short walk from the shuttle buses (allowing you to skip the parking mess and cost).

NORMANDY

$ Les Vieilles Digues, where charming, English-speaking Danielle will pamper you, is two miles toward Pontorson on the main road (on the left if you're coming from Mont St-Michel). It has a lovely garden and six spotless and homey rooms with subtle Asian touches, all with showers (but no Mont St-Michel views). Ground-floor rooms have private patios on the garden (includes good breakfast, easy parking, 68 Route du Mont St-Michel, tel. 02 33 58 55 30, search "Les Vieilles Digues" on www.chambres-hotes. fr, les.vieillesdigues@yahoo.fr). A pedestrian path offers a comfortable walk along the Couesnon River to the shuttle buses.

$ La Jacotière is closest to Mont St-Michel and within walking distance of the regional bus stop and the island shuttle buses (allowing you to avoid all parking fees). Welcoming Véronique offers six immaculate rooms and views of the island from the backyard (studio with great view from private patio, family rooms, includes breakfast, tel. 02 33 60 22 94, www.lajacotiere. fr, la.jacotiere@wanadoo.fr). Drivers coming from Bayeux should turn off the road just prior to the main parking lot. As the road bends to the left away from the bay, look for a regional-products store standing alone on the right. Take the small lane in front of the store signed *sauf véhicule autorisé*—La Jacotière is the next building.

$ Vent des Grèves is about a mile down D-275 from Mont St-Michel (green sign; if arriving from the north, it's just after Auberge de la Baie) and in walking distance to the shuttle buses. Gentle Estelle (who speaks English) and Stéphane (who tries) offer comfortable rooms in two buildings for a steal. The main building has five bright, big, and modern rooms with good views of Mont St-Michel and a common deck with tables to let you soak it all in. The newer section has four sharp rooms in an apartment-like setting with a full living room (includes breakfast, 27 Rue de la Cote, tel. 02 33 48 28 89, www.ventdesgreves.com, ventdesgreves@ orange.fr).

Eating in Mont St-Michel

Puffy omelets (*omelette montoise,* or *omelette tradition*) are Mont St-Michel's specialty. Also look for mussels, seafood platters, and locally raised lamb *pré-salé* (a saltwater-grass diet gives the meat a unique taste, but beware of impostor lamb from New Zealand— ask where your dinner was raised). Muscadet wine (dry, white, and cheap) from the western Loire valley is made nearby and goes well with most regional dishes.

The cuisine served at most restaurants is low quality, similar, and geared to tourists (with *menus* from €18 to €29, cheap crêpes, and full à la carte choices). Pick a restaurant for its view. Window-shop the places that face the bay from the ramparts walk (several access points—one is across from the post office at the bottom of the village) and arrive early to land a view table. Unless noted, the following restaurants are open daily for lunch and dinner.

$$ Hôtel du Guesclin is the top place for a traditional meal, with white tablecloths and beautiful views of the bay from its in-side-only tables (closed Thu, book a window table in advance; see details under "Sleeping in Mont St-Michel—On the Island," earlier).

$$ Restaurant le St. Michel is lighthearted, reasonable, family-friendly, and run by helpful Patricia (decent omelets, mussels, salads, and pasta; open daily for lunch, open for dinner July-Aug, closed Thu-Fri off-season, test its toilet in the rock, across from Hôtel le Mouton Blanc, tel. 02 33 60 14 37).

$$ Café La Mère Poulard is a stylish three-story café-*crê-perie*-restaurant one door up from Hôtel le Mouton Blanc. (Don't confuse it with the Restaurant La Mère Poulard by the drawbridge.) It's worth considering for its upstairs terrace, which offers the best outside table views up to the abbey (when their umbrellas don't block it). **La Vieille Auberge** has a broad terrace with the next-best views to the abbey. **La Croix Blanche** owns a small deck with abbey views and window-front tables with bay views, and **Les Terrasses Poulard** has indoor views to the bay.

Picnics: This is the romantic's choice. The small lanes above the main street hide scenic picnic spots, such as the small park at the base of the ancient treadwheel ramp to the upper abbey. You'll catch late sun by following the ramp that leads you through the *gendarmerie* and down behind the island (on the left as you face the main entry to the island). Sandwiches, pizza by the slice, salads, and drinks are all available to go at shops (open until 19:00) along the main drag. You'll find a better selection at the modest grocery on the mainland (see "Helpful Hints" on page 98).

Mont St-Michel Connections

BY TRAIN, BUS, OR TAXI

Bus and train service to and from Mont St-Michel can be a challenge. You may find that you're forced to arrive and depart early or late—leaving you with too much or too little time on the island. Understand all of your options.

From Mont St-Michel to Paris: Most travelers take the regional bus from Mont St-Michel's parking lot to Rennes and connect directly to a high-speed train (10/day via Rennes, about 3 hours total from Mont St-Michel to Paris' Gare Montparnasse via fastest train from Rennes; €15 for bus to Rennes; not covered by rail pass, buy ticket from driver, all explained in English at www. destination-montstmichel.com). You can also take a short bus ride to Pontorson (see next) to catch the infrequent local train to Paris. Flixbus runs direct service from Mont St-Michel to Paris' Gare de Bercy.

From Mont St-Michel via Pontorson: The nearest train station to Mont St-Michel is five miles away, in Pontorson (called Pontorson/Mont St-Michel). It's connected to Mont St-Michel by bus or by taxi (see details earlier, under "Arrival in Mont St-Michel"). Trains go from Pontorson to Paris (3/day, 5.5 hours, transfer in Caen, St-Malo, or Rennes) and Bayeux (2-3/day, 2 hours; faster by shuttle van—see page 57).

From Mont St-Michel by Bus to Rennes: 4/day direct, 2 hours, tel. 02 99 19 70 70, www.keolis-emeraude.com/en.

Taxis are more expensive, but are helpful when trains and buses don't cooperate. Figure €100 from Mont St-Michel to St-Malo, and €110 to Dinan (50 percent more on Sun and at night).

BY CAR
From Mont St-Michel to St-Malo, Brittany: The direct (and free) freeway route takes 40 minutes. For a scenic drive into Brittany, take the following route: Head to Pontorson, follow *D-19* signs to St-Malo, then look for *St. Malo par la Côte* and join D-797, which leads along *La Route de la Baie* to D-155 and on to the oyster capital of Cancale. In Cancale, keep tracking *St. Malo par la Côte* and *Route de la Baie* signs. You'll be routed  through the town's port (good lunch stop), then emerge on D-201. Take time to savor Pointe du Grouin, then continue west on D-201 as it hugs the coast to St-Malo.

From Mont St-Michel to Bayeux: Take the free and zippy A-84 toward Caen.

PRACTICALITIES

This section covers just the basics on traveling in France (for much more information, see the latest edition of *Rick Steves France*). You'll find free advice on specific topics at www.ricksteves.com/tips.

THE LANGUAGE

In France, it's essential to acknowledge the person before getting down to business. Start any conversation, or enter any shop, by saying: *"Bonjour, madame (or monsieur)."* To ask if they speak English, say, *"Parlez-vous anglais?"*, and hope they speak more English than you speak French (most do). See "Survival Phrases" at the end of this chapter.

MONEY

France uses the euro currency: 1 euro (€) = about $1.20. To convert prices in euros to dollars, add about 20 percent: €20 = about $24, €50 = about $60. (Check www.oanda.com for the latest exchange rates.)

The standard way for travelers to get euros is to withdraw money from an ATM (which locals call a *distributeur*) using a debit or credit card, ideally with a Visa or MasterCard logo. To keep your cash, cards, and valuables safe, wear a money belt.

Before departing, call your bank or credit-card company: Confirm that your card(s) will work overseas, ask about international transaction fees, and alert them that you'll be making withdrawals in Europe. Also ask for the PIN number for your credit card—you may need it for Europe's "chip-and-PIN" payment machines (see below; allow time for your bank to mail your PIN to you).

Dealing with "Chip and PIN": Most credit and debit cards now have chips that authenticate and secure transactions. European cardholders insert their chip card into the payment slot, then enter a PIN. (For most US cards, you provide a signature.) Any American card, whether with a chip or an old-fashioned magnetic stripe, will work at Europe's hotels, restaurants, and shops. But some self-service chip-and-PIN payment machines—such as those at train stations, toll roads, or unattended gas pumps—may not accept your card, even if you know the PIN. If your card won't work, look for a cashier who can process the transaction manually—or pay in cash.

Dynamic Currency Conversion: If merchants or hoteliers offer to convert your purchase price into dollars (called dynamic currency conversion, or DCC), refuse this "service." You'll pay extra in fees for the expensive convenience of seeing your charge in dollars. If an ATM offers to "lock in" or "guarantee" your conversion rate, choose "proceed without conversion." Other prompts might state, "You can be charged in dollars: Press YES for dollars, NO for euros." Always choose the local currency.

STAYING CONNECTED

The simplest solution is to bring your own device—mobile phone, tablet, or laptop—and use it just as you would at home (following the tips below, such as connecting to free Wi-Fi whenever possible).

To call France from a US or Canadian number: Whether you're phoning from a landline, your own mobile phone, or a Skype account, you're making an international call. Dial 011-33 and then the local number, omitting the initial zero. (The 011 is our international access code, and 33 is France's country code.) If dialing from a mobile phone, you can enter + in place of the international access code—press and hold the 0 key.

To call France from a European country: Dial 00-33 followed by the local number, omitting the initial zero. (The 00 is Europe's international access code.)

To call within France: Just dial the local number (including the initial zero).

To call from France to another country: Dial 00 followed by the country code (for example, 1 for the US or Canada), then the area code and number. If you're calling European countries whose phone numbers begin with 0, you'll usually have to omit that 0 when you dial.

Tips: If you bring your own mobile phone, consider getting an international plan; most providers offer a global calling plan that cuts the per-minute cost of phone calls and texts, and a flat-fee data plan.

Use Wi-Fi whenever possible. Most hotels and many cafés offer free Wi-Fi, and you'll likely also find it at tourist information offices, major museums, and public-transit hubs. With Wi-Fi you can use your phone or tablet to make free or inexpensive domes-

Sleep Code

Hotels are classified based on the average price of a standard double room without breakfast in high season.

$$$$	**Splurge:** Most rooms over €250
$$$	**Pricier:** €190-250
$$	**Moderate:** €130-190
$	**Budget:** €70-130
¢	**Backpacker:** Under €70
RS%	**Rick Steves discount**
*	**French hotel rating system** (0-5 stars)

Unless otherwise noted, credit cards are accepted and free Wi-Fi is available; at B&Bs, you'll likely need to pay cash. Comparison-shop by checking prices at several hotels (on each hotel's own website, on a booking site, or by email). For the best deal, book directly with the hotel. If the listing includes **RS%**, request a Rick Steves discount.

tic and international calls via a calling app such as Skype, Face-Time, or Google+ Hangouts. When you can't find Wi-Fi, you can use your cellular network to connect to the Internet, send texts, or make voice calls. When you're done, avoid further charges by manually switching off "data roaming" or "cellular data."

It's possible to stay connected without a mobile device. You can make calls from your hotel (or the rare public phone), and get online using public computers (there's usually one in your hotel lobby). Most hotels charge a high fee for international calls—ask for rates before you dial. For more on phoning, see www.ricksteves.com/phoning. For a one-hour talk on "Traveling with a Mobile Device," see www.ricksteves.com/travel-talks.

SLEEPING

I've categorized my recommended accommodations based on price, indicated with a dollar-sign rating (see sidebar). I recommend reserving rooms in advance, particularly during peak season. Once your dates are set, check the specific price for your preferred stay at several hotels. You can do this either by comparing prices on sites such as Hotels.com or Booking.com, or by checking the hotels' own websites. To get the best deal, contact my family-run hotels directly by phone or email. When you go direct, the owner avoids any third-party commission, giving them wiggle room to offer you a discount, a nicer room, or free breakfast. If you prefer to book online or are considering a hotel chain, it's to your advantage to use the hotel's website.

For complicated requests, send an email with the following information: number and type of rooms; number of nights; arrival date; departure date; and any special requests. Use the European style for writing dates: day/month/year. Hoteliers typically ask for your credit-card number as a deposit.

Some hotels are willing to make a deal to attract guests: Try emailing several hotels to ask for their best price. In general, hotel prices can soften if you do any of the following: offer to pay cash, stay at least three nights, or travel off-season.

The French have a simple hotel-rating system based on amenities (zero through five stars, indicated in this book by * through *****). Two- and three-star hotels are my mainstay. Other accommodation options include bed-and-breakfasts (*chambres d'hôtes,* usually more affordable than hotels), hostels, campgrounds, or even homes (*gîtes,* rented by the week). For a list of over 16,000 *chambres d'hôtes* throughout France, check www.chambres-hotes.fr.

EATING

I've categorized my recommended eateries based on price, indicated with a dollar-sign rating (see sidebar). The cuisine is a highlight of any French adventure. It's sightseeing for your palate. For a formal meal, go to a restaurant. If you want the option of lighter fare (just soup or a sandwich), head for a café or brasserie instead.

French restaurants usually open for dinner at 19:00 and are typically most crowded around 20:30. Last seating is usually about 21:00 or 22:00 (earlier in villages). If a restaurant serves lunch, it generally goes from about 11:30 to 14:00.

In France, an entrée is the first course, and *le plat* or *le plat du jour* is the main course with vegetables. If you ask for the *menu* (muh-noo), you won't get a list of dishes; you'll get a fixed-price meal—usually your choice of three courses (soup, appetizer, or salad; main course with vegetables; and cheese course or dessert). Drinks are extra. Ask for *la carte* (lah kart) if you want to see a menu and order à la carte, like the locals do. Request the waiter's help in deciphering the French.

Cafés and brasseries provide budget-friendly meals. If you're hungry between lunch and dinner, when restaurants are closed, go to a brasserie, which generally serves throughout the day. (Some cafés do as well, but others close their kitchens from 14:00 to 18:00.) Compared to restaurants, cafés and brasseries usually have more limited and inexpensive fare, including salads, sandwiches, omelets, *plats du jour,* and more. Check the price list first, which by law must be posted prominently. There are two sets of prices: You'll pay more for the same drink if you're seated at a table *(salle)* than if you're seated or standing at the bar or counter *(comptoir).*

Tipping: A 12-15 percent service charge *(service compris)* is always included in the bill. Most French never tip, but if you feel the service was exceptional, it's kind to tip up to 5 percent extra.

Restaurant Price Code

I've assigned each eatery a price category, based on the average cost of a typical main course. Drinks, desserts, and splurge items (steak and seafood) can raise the price considerably.

$$$$	**Splurge:** Most main courses over €25
$$$	**Pricier:** €20-25
$$	**Moderate:** €15-20
$	**Budget:** Under €15

In France, a crêpe stand or other takeout spot is **$**; a sit-down brasserie, café, or bistro with affordable *plats du jour* is **$$**; a casual but more upscale restaurant is **$$$**; and a swanky splurge is **$$$$**.

TRANSPORTATION

By Train: Travelers who need to cover long distances in France by train can get a good deal with a Eurail France Pass, sold only outside Europe. To see if a railpass could save you money, check www.ricksteves.com/rail. To research train schedules, visit Germany's excellent all-Europe website, www.bahn.com. The French rail website is www.sncf.com; for online sales, go to http://en.voyages-sncf.com. You can also buy tickets at train-station ticket windows, SNCF boutiques (small, centrally located offices of the national rail company), and travel agencies. Travelers with smartphones have the option of saving tickets and reservations directly to their phones (see http://en.voyages-sncf.com/en/mobile).

All **high-speed TGV trains** in France (also called "InOui") require a seat reservation—book as early as possible, as these trains fill fast, and some routes use TGV trains almost exclusively. This is especially true if you're traveling with a rail pass, as TGV passholder reservations are limited, and usually sell out well before other seat reservations do.

You are required to validate (*composter*, kohm-poh-stay) all train tickets and reservations when printed on official ticket stock; before boarding look for a yellow machine to stamp your ticket or reservation. Reserved tickets that are printed at home on plain paper and etickets on your phone don't need validation. Strikes (*grève*) in France are common but generally last no longer than a day or two; ask your hotelier if one is coming.

By Car: It's cheaper to arrange most car rentals from the US. For tips on your insurance options, see www.ricksteves.com/cdw, and for route planning, consult www.viamichelin.com. Bring your driver's license.

Local road etiquette is similar to that in the US. Ask your car-rental company for details, or check the US State Department website (www.travel.state.gov, search for France in the "Learn about your destination" box, then click on "Travel and Transportation").

France's toll road (*autoroute*) system is slick and speedy, but pricey; four hours of driving costs about €25 in tolls. Be aware that US credit cards may not work in toll machines (use the cash lanes and have coins or bills under €50). Your US credit cards also may not work at self-service gas pumps and automated parking garages—but if you know your PIN, try it anyway. The easiest solution is carrying sufficient cash.

A car is a worthless headache in cities—park it safely (get tips from your hotel or pay to park at well-patrolled lots; look for blue *P* signs). As break-ins are common, be sure your valuables are out of sight and locked in the trunk, or even better, with you or in your hotel room.

By Bus: Regional buses work well for many destinations not served by trains. Buses are almost always comfortable and air-conditioned. For dirt-cheap bus fares between cities in France, check out www.flixbus.com and www.ouibus.com.

HELPFUL HINTS

Emergency Help: In France, dial 112 for any emergency. For English-speaking **police,** dial 17. To summon an **ambulance,** call 15. To replace a passport, call the **US Consulate and Embassy** in Paris (tel. 01 43 12 22 22, 4 Avenue Gabriel, Mo: Concorde, http://france.usembassy.gov) or the **US Consulate** in Marseille (tel. 01 43 12 48 85). Canadians can call the **Canadian Consulate and Embassy** in Paris (tel. 01 44 43 29 02, 35 Avenue Montaigne, Mo: Franklin D. Roosevelt, www.amb-canada.fr) or the **Canadian Consulate** in Nice (tel. 04 93 92 93 22). For other concerns, get advice from your hotelier.

Theft or Loss: France has hardworking pickpockets, and they particularly target those coming in from Paris airports—wear a money belt. Assume beggars are pickpockets and any scuffle is simply a distraction by a team of thieves. If you stop for any commotion or show, put your hands in your pockets before someone else does.

To replace a passport, you'll need to go in person to an embassy or consulate (see above). Cancel and replace your credit and debit cards by calling these 24-hour US numbers collect: Visa—tel. 303/967-1096, MasterCard—tel. 636/722-7111, American Express—tel. 336/393-1111. In France, to make a collect call to the US, dial 08 00 90 06 24 and say "operator" for an English-speaking operator. For another option (with the same results), you can call these toll-free numbers in France: Visa (tel. 08 00 90 11 79) and MasterCard (tel. 08 00 90 13 87). File a police report either on the spot or within a day or two; you'll need it to submit an insurance claim for lost or stolen railpasses or travel gear, and it can help with replacing your passport or credit and debit cards. For more information, see www.ricksteves.com/help.

Time: France uses the 24-hour clock. It's the same through 12:00 noon, then keep going: 13:00, 14:00, and so on. France, like most of continental Europe, is six/nine hours ahead of the East/West Coasts of the US.

Business Hours: Most shops are open from Monday through Saturday (generally 10:00–12:00 & 14:00–19:00) and closed on Sunday, though some grocery stores, bakeries, and street markets are open Sunday morning until noon. In smaller towns, many businesses are closed on Monday until 14:00 and sometimes all day. Touristy shops are usually open daily.

Sights: Opening and closing hours of sights can change unexpectedly; confirm the latest times with the local tourist information office or its website. Some major churches enforce a modest dress code (no bare shoulders or shorts) for everyone, even children.

Holidays and Festivals: France celebrates many holidays, which can close sights and attract crowds (book hotel rooms ahead). For information on holidays and festivals, check France's website: http://us.france.fr. For a simple list showing major—though not all—events, see www.ricksteves.com/festivals.

Numbers and Stumblers: What Americans call the second floor of a building is the first floor in Europe. Europeans write dates as day/month/year, so Christmas 2019 is 25/12/19. Commas are decimal points and vice versa—a dollar and a half is 1,50, a thousand is 1.000, and there are 5.280 feet in a mile. France uses the metric system: A kilogram is 2.2 pounds; a liter is about a quart; and a kilometer is six-tenths of a mile.

RESOURCES FROM RICK STEVES

This Snapshot guide is excerpted from my latest edition of *Rick Steves France,* one of many titles in my ever-expanding series of guidebooks on European travel. I also produce a public television series, *Rick Steves' Europe,* and a public radio show, *Travel with Rick Steves.* My website, www.ricksteves.com, offers free travel information, a forum for travelers' comments, guidebook updates, my travel blog, an online travel store, and information on European railpasses and our tours of Europe. If you're bringing a mobile device, my free Rick Steves Audio Europe app features dozens of self-guided audio tours of the top sights in Europe and travel interviews about France. You can get Rick Steves Audio Europe via Apple's App Store, Google Play, or the Amazon Appstore. For more information, see www.ricksteves.com/audioeurope.

ADDITIONAL RESOURCES

Tourist Information: http://us.france.fr
Passports and Red Tape: www.travel.state.gov
Packing List: www.ricksteves.com/packing
Travel Insurance: www.ricksteves.com/insurance
Cheap Flights: www.kayak.com or www.google.com/flights
Airplane Carry-on Restrictions: www.tsa.gov
Updates for This Book: www.ricksteves.com/update

HOW WAS YOUR TRIP?

To share your tips, concerns, and discoveries after using this book, please fill out the survey at www.ricksteves.com/feedback. Thanks in advance—it helps a lot.

PRACTICALITIES

French Survival Phrases

When using the phonetics, try to nasalize the n̲ sound.

English	French	Pronunciation
Good day.	Bonjour.	boh̲n̲-zhoor
Mrs. / Mr.	Madame / Monsieur	mah-dahm / muhs-yuh
Do you speak English?	Parlez-vous anglais?	par-lay-voo ah̲n̲-glay
Yes. / No.	Oui. / Non.	wee / noh̲n̲
I understand.	Je comprends.	zhuh koh̲n̲-prah̲n̲
I don't understand.	Je ne comprends pas.	zhuh nuh koh̲n̲-prah̲n̲ pah
Please.	S'il vous plaît.	see voo play
Thank you.	Merci.	mehr-see
I'm sorry.	Désolé.	day-zoh-lay
Excuse me.	Pardon.	par-doh̲n̲
(No) problem.	(Pas de) problème.	(pah duh) proh-blehm
It's good.	C'est bon.	say boh̲n̲
Goodbye.	Au revoir.	oh ruh-vwahr
one / two	un / deux	uh̲n̲ / duh
three / four	trois / quatre	trwah / kah-truh
five / six	cinq / six	sa̲n̲k / sees
seven / eight	sept / huit	seht / weet
nine / ten	neuf / dix	nuhf / dees
How much is it?	Combien?	koh̲n̲-bee-a̲n̲
Write it?	Ecrivez?	ay-kree-vay
Is it free?	C'est gratuit?	say grah-twee
Included?	Inclus?	a̲n̲-klew
Where can I buy / find...?	Où puis-je acheter / trouver...?	oo pwee-zhuh ah-shuh-tay / troo-vay
I'd like / We'd like...	Je voudrais / Nous voudrions...	zhuh voo-dray / noo voo-dree-oh̲n̲
...a room.	...une chambre.	ewn shah̲n̲-bruh
...a ticket to ___.	...un billet pour ___.	uh̲n̲ bee-yay poor ___
Is it possible?	C'est possible?	say poh-see-bluh
Where is...?	Où est...?	oo ay
...the train station	...la gare	lah gar
...the bus station	...la gare routière	lah gar root-yehr
...tourist information	...l'office du tourisme	loh-fees dew too-reez-muh
Where are the toilets?	Où sont les toilettes?	oo soh̲n̲ lay twah-leht
men	hommes	ohm
women	dames	dahm
left / right	à gauche / à droite	ah gohsh / ah drwaht
straight	tout droit	too drwah
When does this open / close?	Ça ouvre / ferme à quelle heure?	sah oo-vruh / fehrm ah kehl ur
At what time?	À quelle heure?	ah kehl ur
Just a moment.	Un moment.	uh̲n̲ moh-mah̲n̲
now / soon / later	maintenant / bientôt / plus tard	ma̲n̲-tuh-nah̲n̲ / bee-a̲n̲-toh / plew tar
today / tomorrow	aujourd'hui / demain	oh-zhoor-dwee / duh-ma̲n̲

In a French Restaurant

PRACTICALITIES

English	French	Pronunciation
I'd like / We'd like...	Je voudrais / Nous voudrions...	zhuh voo-dray / noo voo-dree-oh<u>n</u>
...to reserve...	...réserver...	ray-zehr-vay
...a table for one / two.	...une table pour un / deux.	ewn tah-bluh poor uh<u>n</u> / duh
Is this seat free?	C'est libre?	say lee-bruh
The menu (in English), please.	La carte (en anglais), s'il vous plaît.	lah kart (ah<u>n</u> ah<u>n</u>-glay) see voo play
service (not) included	service (non) compris	sehr-vees (noh<u>n</u>) koh<u>n</u>-pree
to go	à emporter	ah ah<u>n</u>-por-tay
with / without	avec / sans	ah-vehk / sah<u>n</u>
and / or	et / ou	ay / oo
special of the day	plat du jour	plah dew zhoor
specialty of the house	spécialité de la maison	spay-see-ah-lee-tay duh lah may-zoh<u>n</u>
appetizers	hors d'oeuvre	or duh-vruh
first course (soup, salad)	entrée	ah<u>n</u>-tray
main course (meat, fish)	plat principal	plah pra<u>n</u>-see-pahl
bread	pain	pa<u>n</u>
cheese	fromage	froh-mahzh
sandwich	sandwich	sahnd-weech
soup	soupe	soop
salad	salade	sah-lahd
meat	viande	vee-ahnd
chicken	poulet	poo-lay
fish	poisson	pwah-soh<u>n</u>
seafood	fruits de mer	frwee duh mehr
fruit	fruit	frwee
vegetables	légumes	lay-gewm
dessert	dessert	day-sehr
mineral water	eau minérale	oh mee-nay-rahl
tap water	l'eau du robinet	loh dew roh-bee-nay
milk	lait	lay
(orange) juice	jus (d'orange)	zhew (doh-rah<u>n</u>zh)
coffee / tea	café / thé	kah-fay / tay
wine	vin	va<u>n</u>
red / white	rouge / blanc	roozh / blah<u>n</u>
glass / bottle	verre / bouteille	vehr / boo-tay
beer	bière	bee-ehr
Cheers!	Santé!	sah<u>n</u>-tay
More. / Another.	Plus. / Un autre.	plew / uhn oh-truh
The same.	La même chose.	lah mehm shohz
The bill, please.	L'addition, s'il vous plaît.	lah-dee-see-oh<u>n</u> see voo play
Do you accept credit cards?	Vous prenez les cartes?	voo pruh-nay lay kart
tip	pourboire	poor-bwahr
Delicious!	Délicieux!	day-lees-yuh

For more user-friendly French phrases, check out *Rick Steves' French Phrase Book and Dictionary* or *Rick Steves' French, Italian & German Phrase Book*.

INDEX

INDEX

Explore Europe

At ricksteves.com you can browse through thousands of articles, videos, photos and radio interviews, plus find a wealth of money-saving travel tips for planning your dream trip. And with our mobile-friendly website, you can easily access all this great travel information anywhere you go.

TV Shows

Preview the places you'll visit by watching entire half-hour episodes of Rick Steves' Europe (choose from all 100 shows) on-demand, for free.

your travel dreams into affordable reality

Radio Interviews

Enjoy ready access to Rick's vast library of radio interviews covering travel

tips and cultural insights that relate specifically to your Europe travel plans.

Travel Forums

Learn, ask, share! Our online community of savvy travelers is a great resource

for first-time travelers to Europe, as well as seasoned pros. You'll find forums on each country, plus travel tips and restaurant/hotel reviews. You can even ask one of our well-traveled staff to chime in with an opinion.

Travel News

Subscribe to our free Travel News e-newsletter, and get monthly updates from Rick on what's happening in Europe.

Rick's Free Travel App

Get your FREE **Rick Steves Audio Europe**™ app to enjoy…

- Dozens of self-guided tours of Europe's top museums, sights and historic walks
- Hundreds of tracks filled with cultural insights and sightseeing tips from Rick's radio interviews
- All organized into handy geographic playlists
- For Apple and Android

With Rick whispering in your ear, Europe gets even better.

Find out more at ricksteves.com

Gear up for your next adventure at ricksteves.com

Light Luggage

Pack light and right with Rick Steves' affordable, custom-designed rolling carry-on bags, backpacks, day packs and shoulder bags.

Accessories

From packing cubes to moneybelts and beyond, Rick has personally selected the travel goodies that will help your trip go smoother.

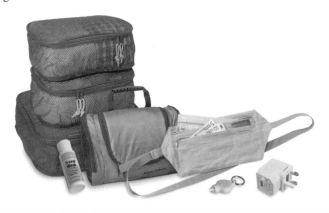

Experience maximum Europe

Save time and energy

This guidebook is your independent-travel toolkit. But for all it delivers, it's still up to you to devote the time and energy it takes to manage the preparation and logistics that are essential for a happy trip. If that's a hassle, there's a solution.

Rick Steves Tours

A Rick Steves tour takes you to Europe's most interesting places with great

with minimum stress

guides and small groups of 28 or less. We follow Rick's favorite itineraries, ride in comfy buses, stay in family-run hotels, and bring you intimately

close to the Europe you've traveled so far to see. Most importantly, we take away the logistical headaches so you can focus on the fun.

travelers—nearly half of them repeat customers— along with us on four dozen different itineraries, from Ireland to Italy to Athens. Is a Rick Steves tour the right fit for your travel dreams? Find out at ricksteves.com, where you can also request Rick's latest tour catalog. Europe is best experienced with happy travel partners. We hope you can join us.

Join the fun

This year we'll take thousands of free-spirited

See our itineraries at ricksteves.com

A Guide for Every Trip

BEST OF GUIDES

Full color easy-to-scan format, focusing on Europe's most popular destinations and sights.

Best of France
Best of Germany
Best of England
Best of Europe
Best of Ireland
Best of Italy
Best of Spain

COMPREHENSIVE GUIDES

City, country, and regional guides with detailed coverage for a multi-week trip exploring the most iconic sights and venturing off the beaten track.

Amsterdam & the Netherlands
Barcelona
Belgium: Bruges, Brussels, Antwerp & Ghent
Berlin
Budapest
Croatia & Slovenia
Eastern Europe
England
Florence & Tuscany
France
Germany
Great Britain
Greece: Athens & the Peloponnese
Iceland
Ireland
Istanbul
Italy
London
Paris
Portugal
Prague & the Czech Republic
Provence & the French Riviera
Rome
Scandinavia
Scotland
Spain
Switzerland
Venice
Vienna, Salzburg & Tirol

THE BEST OF ROME

ome, Italy's capital, is studded with
oman remnants and floodlit-fountain
uares. From the Vatican to the Colos-
um, with crazy traffic in between, Rome
onderful, huge, and exhausting. The
wds, the heat, and the weighty history

of the Eternal City where Caesars walked
can make tourists wilt. Recharge by taking siestas, gelato breaks, and after-dark
walks, strolling from one atmospheric
square to another in the refreshing evening air.

ired **Pantheon**—which
gest dome until the
arly 2,000 years old
day over 1,500).

al of Athens in the **Vat**-
bodies the humanistic
ance.

, gladiators fought
another, entertaining
0.

his Rome **ristorante**.

rds at **St. Peter's**
k seriously.

in, toss in a coin
turn to Rome, tat

Rick Steves guidebooks are published by Avalon Travel,
an imprint of Perseus Books, a Hachette Book Group compan

POCKET GUIDES

Compact, full color city guides with the essentials for shorter trips.

Amsterdam
Athens
Barcelona
Florence
Italy's Cinque Terre
London
Munich & Salzburg

Paris
Prague
Rome
Venice
Vienna

SNAPSHOT GUIDES

Focused single-destination coverage.

Basque Country: Spain & France
Copenhagen & the Best of Denmark
Dublin
Dubrovnik
Edinburgh
Hill Towns of Central Italy
Krakow, Warsaw & Gdansk
Lisbon
Loire Valley
Madrid & Toledo
Milan & the Italian Lakes District
Naples & the Amalfi Coast
Northern Ireland
Normandy
Norway
Reykjavik
Sevilla, Granada & Southern Spain
St. Petersburg, Helsinki & Tallinn
Stockholm

CRUISE PORTS GUIDES

Reference for cruise ports of call.

Mediterranean Cruise Ports
Northern European Cruise Ports

Complete your library with...

TRAVEL SKILLS & CULTURE

Study up on travel skills and gain insight on history and culture.

Europe 101
European Christmas
European Easter
European Festivals
Europe Through the Back Door
Postcards from Europe
Travel as a Political Act

PHRASE BOOKS & DICTIONARIES

French
French, Italian & German
German
Italian
Portuguese
Spanish

PLANNING MAPS

Britain, Ireland & London
Europe
France & Paris
Germany, Austria & Switzerland
Ireland
Italy
Spain & Portugal

Avalon Travel
Hachette Book Group
1700 Fourth Street
Berkeley, CA 94710

Printed in Canada by Friesens.
Fourth Edition. First printing February 2018.

ISBN 978-1-63121-678-7

For the latest on Rick's lectures, guidebooks, tours, public television series, and public radio show, contact Rick Steves' Europe, 130 Fourth Avenue North, Edmonds, WA 98020, 425/771-8303, rick@ricksteves.com, www.ricksteves.com.

Rick Steves' Europe
Managing Editor: Jennifer Madison Davis
Special Publications Manager: Risa Laib
Assistant Managing Editor: Cathy Lu
Editors: Glenn Eriksen, Julie Fanselow, Tom Griffin, Katherine Gustafson, Suzanne Kotz, Rosie Leutzinger, Carrie Shepherd
Editorial & Production Assistant: Jessica Shaw
Researchers: Trish Feaster, Virginie Moré
Contributor: Gene Openshaw
Graphic Content Director: Sandra Hundacker
Maps & Graphics: David C. Hoerlein, Lauren Mills, Mary Rostad

Avalon Travel
Senior Editor and Series Manager: Madhu Prasher
Editor: Jamie Andrade
Associate Editor: Sierra Machado
Copy Editor: Maggie Ryan
Proofreader: Kelly Lydick
Indexer: Stephen Callahan
Production & Typesetting: Christine DeLorenzo, Krista Anderson, Lisi Baldwin, Jane Musser
Cover Design: Kimberly Glyder Design
Maps & Graphics: Kat Bennett

Photo Credits
Front Cover: Alsace © SIME/eStock Photo
Title Page: Along the Seine © Dominic Arizona Bonuccelli
Additional Photography: Dominic Arizona Bonuccelli, Abe Bringolf, Mary Ann Cameron, Julie Coen, Rich Earl, Barb Geisler, Cameron Hewitt, David C. Hoerlein, Michaelanne Jerome, Lauren Mills, Virginie Moré, Gene Openshaw, Paul Orcutt, Rhonda Pelikan, Michael Potter, Carol Ries, Steve Smith, Robyn Stencil, Rick Steves, Gretchen Strauch, Rob Unck, Laura VanDeventer, Dorian Yates, Wikimedia Commons (PD-Art/PD-US). Photos are used by permission and are the property of the original copyright owners.

ABOUT THE AUTHORS

RICK STEVES

Since 1973, Rick has spent about four months a year exploring Europe. His mission: to empower Americans to have European trips that are fun, affordable, and culturally broadening. Rick produces a best-selling guidebook series, a public television series, and a public radio show, and organizes small-group tours that take over 20,000 travelers to Europe annually. He does all of this with the help of a hardworking, well-traveled staff of 100 at Rick Steves' Europe in Edmonds, Washington, near Seattle. When not on the road, Rick is active in his church and with advocacy groups focused on economic justice, drug policy reform, and ending hunger. To recharge, Rick plays piano, relaxes at his family cabin in the Cascade Mountains, and spends time with his partner Trish, son Andy, and daughter Jackie. Find out more about Rick at www.ricksteves.com and on Facebook.

STEVE SMITH

Steve Smith has lived in France on several occasions, starting when he was very young. He restored a farmhouse on the Burgundy canal and still hangs his beret there in research season. Steve has managed guides for Rick Steves' Europe's tour programs and researched guidebooks with Rick for more than two decades. He now focuses his time on guidebooks and exploring every corner of his favorite country. Karen Lewis Smith—an expert on French cuisine and wine—provides invaluable contributions to his books.

Want more France?
Maximize the experience with Rick Steves as your guide

Guidebooks
Provence and Paris guides make side-trips smooth and affordable

Phrase Books
Rely on Rick's French Phrase Book & Dictionary

Rick's TV Shows
Preview your destinations with 12 shows on France

Free! Rick's Audio Europe™ App
Get free audio tours for Paris' top sights

Small Group Tours
Rick offers several great itineraries through France

For all the details, visit ricksteves.com